# BLINDSIDED

# BLINDSIDED

The True Story of One Man's Crusade
Against Chemical Giant DuPont
for a Boy With No Eyes

JAMES L. FERRARO
WITH LAURA MORTON

gildanpress

gildanpress

Published 2017 by Gildan Press
an imprint of Gildan Media LLC.
www.gildanmedia.com

Distributed through the Book Market by Hachette Book Group, USA

FIRST EDITION: 2017

Front cover image: Olga Bogatyrenko/Shutterstock.com.
Back cover image: Fotokostic/Shutterstock.com.

Designed by Meghan Day Healey of Story Horse, LLC
Book packaged by Laura Morton Management

Library of Congress Cataloging-in-Publication Data is available upon request.

ISBN: 978-1-469-03600-7      **33614080409724**

Manufactured in the United States of America by LSC Communications

10   9   8   7   6   5   4   3   2

*Blindsided* is first and foremost dedicated to my late father, Lou, and his ancestors who immigrated, sacrificed, worked tirelessly, and in many cases suffered for the future benefit of their family. I thank my father for instilling in me a strong work ethic and a profound sense of caring and concern for others. Without him, I would not have had the courage to take on a just but difficult cause like the Castillo family faced.

*Blindsided* is also dedicated to the Castillo family with a heavy heart knowing that my work did not give Johnny Castillo the gift of seeing the wonders of our magnificent world. I merely hope that the circumstance of our lives crossing paths made a difference for Johnny and his family by achieving justice for them and the ability to meet many of his special needs.

Finally, I dedicate this book to all those who have been harmed or will be harmed by the reckless behavior of certain corporations that value profits over people. Unfortunately, most of these people will never get their day in court.

# Acknowledgments

I WANT TO thank my children James, Andrew, and Alexis for accepting me for who I am and for putting up with my idiosyncrasies and sometimes eccentric behavior throughout the years. You are my inspiration and my driving force to make the world a better place. I also want to thank my sons, Dmitri and Mateo, my two little angels, who came into my life in the last five years.

I would be nowhere without my immediate family, my grandmother, Mary (who is 105!), my mother Luella, brother, John and sister, Kim. In particular, I want to thank you mom, for being a great wife to dad and a perfect mother. I cherish each and every memory of our immediate family living together under one roof. I also want to apologize to my ex-wife, Diane (mother of my first three) for all the trials and tribulations we experienced while living through the early years of the DuPont litigation and for all of my other shenanigans. I want to also thank my fiancée, Megan, who has supported me throughout the writing of this book.

Personally, and professionally, I want to acknowledge the late Michael Kelley and the late Ron Motley. I formed one of my law firms, Kelley & Ferraro, with Michael in 1997. He was my best friend for life and a business partner beyond anyone's dreams. I met Ron in 1989 and he became a great inspiration for me. Ron was a pioneer in asbestos litigation, taking on the tobacco industry, and later seeking compensation for the victims of 9/11.

I also want to thank all my friends, partners, associates, employees and colleagues at The Ferraro Law Firm, which I founded in 1985 in Miami, with offices today located in Florida and Washington DC. I also want to thank all my friends, partners, associates, employees and colleagues at Kelley & Ferraro.

Since the Supreme Court of Florida ruled on Castillo in 2003, many people encouraged me to share this story. The best reason I could think of to do that would be if the story could help make a positive impact and affect meaningful and significant changes in the system. It took many years to get my words and thoughts down on the page, but the time finally felt right. Sadly, not much has changed since the Castillo trial to prohibit products such as Benlate from getting to the market. Similar agricultural products are being used every day. And, whether we know it or not, there is no doubt, irreversible damage is being done.

I want to thank everyone on my team at Ferraro Law and my close circle of friends who helped make this book become a reality. Without you, *Blindsided* would still be an idea and great cocktail conversation.

I cannot say enough about my co-author Laura Morton, an accomplished writer with 20 *New York Times* best sellers. As an attorney, I was used to writing legal briefs so I wasn't sure Laura would be able to wrap her arms around this story and the legal intricacies it involved. But when we met, she alleviated that doubt right away. I needed someone to convert my legalese into layman's terms. Laura, you were definitely the one. Adam Mitchell, your research, insight and assistance on this project was invaluable. Hope Innelli, you are the consummate professional. Your editorial intuition and expertise is second to none and helped take this book from good to great. Meghan Day Healey, your creativity and design work on the cover and interior is top shelf. You understood the vision from the start and carried it throughout the entire process with grace and ease. A big thank you goes to Jan Forzano, and the entire team at our printer, LSC Communications. I also want to thank Gilles Dana, President and Publisher of Gildan Media and Ellen Goldberg, Managing Editor for Gildan Media, for believing in this book from the very start. I want to thank Christian Slater for his friendship and incredibly generous contribution in reading the audio for *Blindsided*. I also want to thank Joan Lunden, Alan Dershowitz and Judge Donner for their support on this project. And, to everyone at Hachette for their support in sales and marketing including Todd McGarity, Vanessa Vazquez Watts and Billy Clark.

And finally, to all those who have gone up against their own Goliath. Those who weren't afraid to take a stand for what they believed in with such passion they somehow made a difference, leaving their mark and making a difference in the world for all of us. One voice can make a difference.

# BLINDSIDED

# Introduction
## June 1993

IT WAS ANOTHER habitually late night in the office when I heard my private phone line ring. I was working on an important and time-consuming case. Although I rarely answer my own calls, even after hours, for some reason I reached for the receiver.

"Hello?"

"Hercules. How ya doin', man? Look, before you say anything, I have a favor to ask."

It was my longtime friend Mark Eichberg. We first met in college and became good friends back in the early 1980s when I was an accountant. He and I used to work out together a lot, so we started calling each other Hercules.

"What's up, Hercules?"

"Listen, I work with this guy, Juan Castillo. He and his wife are desperate to hire a lawyer. You've got to see them, man, and hear them out."

The truth is, I hated getting these types of calls. They usually led to some bullshit case in which I had to explain to the family sitting across from me all the reasons why they had no claim or recourse in the judicial system. I didn't like being the bad guy delivering that kind of news. I understood how personal these situations were to people. I dealt with them every day. But I also knew the process, and most of the time it wasn't anything like the glorified, glamorous version we all see on TV. Besides, it wasn't as if I was hard up for work; in just a few years, my small law firm had grown exponentially. I went from representing a hundred people to advocating for several thousand in liability cases largely related to asbestos-induced diseases such as mesothelioma, lung cancer and asbestosis. I'd also done some work on a variety of medical malpractice cases, mostly representing the plaintiffs. These cases were often hard to win, but that's what made trying them so appealing to me. I enjoy a good challenge, and in a field where a lot of my colleagues tend to stick with the same kinds of clients and cases, I appreciated the difficulty in pursuing different types of cases. From a lawyer's point of view—or at least from my personal perspective—there's nothing more exciting than building a case piece by piece, convincing a jury you are right, and then having them put a high dollar value on something as painful as watching someone you love suffer long and hard before they eventually die from the disease in question, or in many cases enduring that pain themselves before they die. This is my art—an art that takes a great deal of skill, thoughtful strategy, and determined precision to win.

And I love to win.

Yeah, business was booming. I didn't have the time or the interest to take on dead-end cases. Even so, Mark wasn't the kind of friend I could say no to, so I reluctantly agreed to set up a meeting with the couple he was referring to me.

1

WHEN DONNA CASTILLO first walked into my office, she struck me as demure and fairly typical of the people I met and represented every day. Her husband, Juan, a Cuban American, worked as an accountant at a pension company. Donna was a former schoolteacher born and raised in Massachusetts. She had sandy brown hair and spoke with a thick New England accent. She and Juan met in Florida and had made a home for their family in Kendall. At the time, the area was part of unincorporated Dade County, which was comprised of mostly farmland. I used to go for long runs out that way in the early '80s, so I knew the city well. As Donna began to share more about her life, she spoke of her and Juan's two young children, a six-year-old girl named Adrianna and their three-year-old boy, John. She described what appeared to be a very loving, close-knit family, although I could tell there was a painful, underlying strain there. You could see it in her eyes.

"Tell me why you're here today," I said.

Donna spoke softly as she did her best to fight back tears. She told me that on approximately the first or second of November 1989, she had decided to take her young daughter for a walk in her stroller to get some fresh air. As they passed by Pine Island Farms, a typical "u-pick" field usually full of strawberries and tomatoes, she noticed that a tractor had become stuck in the mud. The sprayer attachment had a big wingspan, close to thirty-six feet end to end, and it was spraying a clear, odorless liquid as it thrashed uncontrollably about. She stopped for a brief moment and watched the driver of the tractor try unsuccessfully to maneuver the vehicle out of the soaked ground. It was a relatively windy day, and at one point the gusts shifted in such a way that Donna became wet from the spray. Since the liquid didn't have any noticeable color, smell, or taste, she assumed it was just water. She was eight or nine weeks pregnant, and though she wasn't terribly concerned at the time, she went home and shared her experience with her husband. He agreed that there was probably nothing to be worried about.

Just to be certain, she went to the obstetrician the next day. After listening to the details of her encounter, the doctor came to the same conclusion. The farmer must have been watering his crop, as there was no obvious evidence of any chemical use.

Seven months later, Donna gave birth to her son, John. She and Juan had expected a perfectly healthy child because there had been no sign of any problems throughout the pregnancy. The reality in the delivery room, however, was quite different. The couple was horrified to learn that John was born with no eyes. They had no idea what had caused this rare birth defect. In time, I would learn that when a child is born with no eyes, the condition is known as anophthalmia. Similarly, when a child is born with only residual tissue in place of his or her eyes or with abnormally small eyes, this sister condition to anophthalmia is called microphthalmia. Although Johnny had no eyes, he did have a tiny cyst where his eyes should have been; thus, his condition was classified as microphthalmia.

"The condition is incurable," Donna said, now sobbing as she pulled a small photo of the baby from her purse.

She told me that while Johnny could someday be fitted with glass prosthetic eyes, he would never be able to see. Not only would he be blind for life, he was permanently disfigured.

This discovery was shocking to the Castillos. They certainly weren't prepared for life with a blind child. The condition is so rare that they wanted to find answers. What could have caused this? Was it something Donna could have prevented? Was it genetic? She told me about a British support group she became involved with called Microphthalmia, Anophthalmia & Coloboma Support, also known as MACS. There were 165 other families enduring a similar journey, and she found great support and comfort through their mutual connection.

As I listened to Donna share her story, I couldn't help but think of my own son Andrew. He was the same age as little Johnny. I glanced at my boy's photo, which sat in a frame on my desk. There he was, a beautiful, healthy kid. I got to go home every day and see him, and by the grace of God, he got to *see* me, too. I couldn't fathom what life would be like if any of my children—Andrew; my oldest son James, who was then seven; or my daughter, Alexis, who had been born just months earlier in January—were suffering the way Johnny was. My heart was genuinely broken for the Castillo family. They were humble people. Good people. I could see the anguish this had caused them. And yet I still wasn't sure why they were sitting in my office that day.

"I'm sorry about your son, I really am; but I'm still unclear as to why you're here," I said. I wanted to be compassionate and understanding, but I'm a trial lawyer, not a therapist.

That's when Donna told me about an investigation the *London Observer* and the BBC were both conducting. It was focused on a cluster of kids born without eyes in Fife, Scotland. They all lived in an agricultural area where farmers frequently used a chemical called carbendazim. Although sold under a different trade name, this chemical is similar to one made by DuPont called benomyl, the active ingredient in a product known as Benlate. At the time, Benlate was the best-selling and most profitable agricultural product DuPont was selling worldwide. Pregnant women working with these products—primarily migrant workers—were giving birth to children with Johnny's affliction. A 1993 documentary called *Field of Dreams* followed the stories of these women and their children. John Ashton, an investigative reporter from the *Observer*, was digging deeper into the subject, contacting farmers and families to see if he could connect the dots. He got in touch with Donna and asked if she had lived near any farms when she was pregnant with John.

She had.

He asked if she had ever been sprayed by a foreign substance near one of those farms.

She had.

Donna said that after she gave Ashton all the details of that fateful day, it suddenly occurred to her that she, too, may have been the victim of this type of chemical exposure.

When Ashton followed up on Donna's story with Lynn Chaffin, a field manager from the farm where Donna had been walking on the first or second of November 1989, he asked if Benlate had been used on the field crops on or about that date.

Chaffin said yes.

This would be a pivotal piece of evidence if there were to be a case going forward.

I suddenly understood why the Castillos were in my office that day.

They wanted to go after DuPont.

Holy shit.

In 1991 Benlate was alleged to be contaminated with another DuPont product, weed killer sulfonylurea, which was the most potent herbicide known to agriculture. More than 2,100 growers nationwide said that tainted Benlate ruined millions of dollars in plants and left thousands of acres of land unusable. DuPont paid more than $510 million in damage claims until it abruptly stopped payments after it said its own tests showed Benlate could not have damaged plants. The grower's lawyers said that DuPont had defrauded both growers and Federal regulators by hiding its knowledge about the product's defects.

While this case showed their product caused harm to plants I had never heard of it doing damage to people—or, more specifically, causing harm to unborn embryos and fetuses.

At least, that was the case before the Castillos entered the picture.

There had never been a jury verdict rendered anywhere in the entire world against a chemical-producing corporate giant like DuPont for developing products that caused birth defects of any type.

It was now clear why every other lawyer the Castillos went to before me had turned them away.

They didn't stand a chance of going the distance against a behemoth like that. They surely didn't have the money or the stamina it would take to stare down DuPont, let alone win. They needed someone stupid enough to take the case and then finance it, too.

At the time, I was well on my way to becoming a wildly successful trial lawyer. But I was a bit of an oddity. I say that because all the successful trial lawyers I've ever known or heard of began their careers working under a mentor.

I didn't.

I started my law firm two years out of law school and was never mentored by anyone. I would learn to prepare my witnesses, opening statements, and closing arguments by reading books and memoirs by the legendary trial lawyers of the past.

I would simply take what I liked from one, add it to what I liked from another, and then layer a little bit of my own insight on top.

Maybe not having a mentor to talk me out of it is what made me both naive and brazen enough to take on a case like the Castillos'. I was free to do it if I wanted. I didn't have to answer to anyone else.

Besides, at the time I was also very idealistic—almost to a fault.

I consider myself very lucky to have represented so many people who didn't stand a chance to win without me. I've not only helped change the lives of those people but I've also had the good fortune to make a lot of money doing it.

Naive or not, one thing was very clear after hearing Donna's story: everybody on the street is a potential victim of chemical exposure like Donna endured that day. By not even thinking about the potential damage they were causing, DuPont—and the farmers using their products—were operating with a total disregard for the public. Worse, they didn't seem to care. If the DuPonts of the world had their way, everyone would be considered human guinea pigs, much like the Castillos were. The biggest problem this beleaguered family faced was proving it.

Chemical cases involving birth defects are almost impossible to prove. While human test trials are done to determine whether a new drug is beneficial or harmful to people, there are no such trials for chemicals. The reason is very basic: no possible good can come from testing chemicals on humans, and in particular on pregnant women. It is simply unethical to perform such tests.

This is the challenge with Benlate and benomyl. You simply can't spray potentially dangerous chemicals meant to kill weeds or enhance crop growth on pregnant women to see what will happen to their unborn children. There's absolutely nothing positive that can result from a study like that. Because there is no possible benefit, human test trials—which would be the best indicators of potential birth defects—are not only unethical, they're prohibited.

By comparison, when a pharmaceutical company screws up and damage to humans results from one of their drugs, it's much easier to build a case against them, because data can be gathered from the controlled human test trials they typically run. It's allowable to test new drugs on humans because it is generally understood that the possible benefits outweigh the risks. For example, when it comes to treating cancer, the prevailing view is that any new drug with the potential to kill the deadly cancer cells is well worth testing even if some people will be harmed in the process. Such trials are critical to moving medicine forward, which makes them invaluable.

That is very sound reasoning. With chemicals, however, the only allowable testing is on human cadaver skin and cells (not living people), and on animals. This plays right into the hands of the DuPonts of the world. It makes it very easy for them to be irresponsible. This inherent limitation in testing makes it possible for companies with potentially toxic and harmful products to get away with selling them to the unsuspecting public. Even when faced with living examples of severe human damage, companies such as DuPont are willing to sacrifice a thousand Johnny Castillos before they'll toss in the towel. They believe they should be able to sell their products, toxic or not, with very little regulation.

I was curious about how a victory against a behemoth like DuPont would impact this family. How would it make their lives different? Donna explained that if they won, Johnny could get the education, develop the skills, undergo the therapy, and secure the devices necessary to meet his special needs. This would make his life much more bearable.

"Juan doesn't make that much money, and our wish—our hope—is to send our son to the Perkins School for the Blind," she said.

I knew the Perkins School was very expensive. There was no shot of little Johnny going there unless they won this case.

As I held Johnny's photo in my hand, again I found myself thinking about my own children. I wondered what I would do if this were my son. I admit, this case represented everything I loved about being a lawyer.

I wasn't as humble as the Castillos.

I'd want vindication by proving this company had fucked up. I'd want to show the court that, without any question, it wasn't something my wife did that caused my child's condition. It wasn't her mistake, but rather the fault of someone who thought they could get away with causing this type of harm because they weren't being held accountable for it.

Shit.

This family needed me.

It would be challenging, make no mistake about it—this was a real-life David-and-Goliath battle we were about to wage.

It would take a miracle to win.

And it had my name written all over it.

"Let me get this straight," I said. "You're asking me if I'll represent you against DuPont?"

Donna stared back at me, wiping away her tears with a handful of tissues she took from the box on my desk. She appeared so helpless.

"Yes, Mr. Ferraro. That is why I'm here," she said quietly.

I sat still for a moment, contemplating my next move. I looked at Donna, who was so sad. I'm not good when people cry. I'm a sucker at pity parties and usually play right into them, especially when it comes to women. But this was different. In this case, I genuinely felt empathy for Donna and her husband. I wouldn't want to be in their shoes or trade the good fortune I had with my three healthy children for the challenging life they faced with their daughter and sightless son.

There have been many times in my career when I've wanted to take on cases despite the fact that I knew they were unwinnable. Times when I was sure an injustice had occurred but suspected the odds were against me. Times, for instance, when multiple companies were dumping toxic waste in the same place, so there was no way to prove whose fault it was. Times when I had the desire to be a hero but still had to tell victims who'd suffered horrific consequences to get on with their lives even though their time was surely limited and their quality of life would never be the same. That doesn't get any easier for me. And yet sometimes it's the only advice I can offer, because there is no other solution.

I started to give Donna my usual spiel. I wanted to encourage her and Juan to put this ordeal behind them and move on with their lives.

I explained that sometimes things happen, and we may never understand the reason or purpose. These are things that are out of our control. They're in God's hands, and we have to trust in Him. But that wasn't the way the Castillos' story would end.

I knew it, and so did they.

I was doing my best to sound compassionate and sympathetic. Even as I spoke, I felt something rising inside me. I recognized that nagging feeling I get when a grave injustice has been done, the certainty that I can make a difference in someone's life if we pursue a case together. But I didn't want to drag the Castillos into a five-year battle they would most likely lose. It would be the worst emotional roller coaster they'd ever go on. I knew that. I sincerely didn't want to engage them in the battle if they couldn't win the war. That's what happens. People become so obsessed with the fight along the way that they run the risk of being totally devastated by the final outcome. I understood it was a difficult, if not impossible case at best, and yet if I didn't take this chance, I was certain no one else would either. The family had already been to several much larger law firms—firms that could bankroll a case like this with more ease than I could—and were turned down by every one of them. It was lunacy for me to take this on. This situation seemed to shout, "Run for the hills!" but still I found myself running toward the Castillos rather than away from them.

I knew this case could potentially take years to win. I also knew it would cost my firm hundreds of thousands, if not millions of dollars to prepare—money I was likely never to see again. One thing was for sure: it would definitely be a long, uphill climb.

Still, something inside told me I had to say yes. I liked taking on new cases that would be interesting, stimulating, and different. It made my job a lot more exhilarating. Also, I liked the competitive challenge of entering groundbreaking territory, especially when I took on cases that everybody else said no to.

Where's the glory in taking on another case exactly like the last one you won? To me, there is none. That kind of path creates complacency and laziness. There was no precedent here, no road map to follow for a case like the one the Castillo family presented. No one had ever taken on a case like it and won before me, and, frankly, no one's been able to repeat that success since.

The Castillo family finally had someone who would fight on their behalf.

Yeah, I was their guy.

"Here's what we're going to do. I'll look to see if there's any science out there to support us. It's going to be very difficult to make what's called an actual-knowledge case against DuPont." I explained that an "actual-knowledge" case requires us to prove that DuPont actually knew how bad this chemical was, yet still allowed it to be sold and used. They would lie their asses off—they'd cover up and hide any corporate knowledge they had. However, there's another way to build and win a case like this in certain states. I'm licensed to practice in several states, and thankfully, Florida is one of those states. Florida allows litigators to argue a "state-of-the art" case. In a state-of-the-art case, companies like DuPont are expected to have expert knowledge of how bad their product is based on the state of the art or science that exists at the time they manufacture, sell, or distribute the product. Since they designed and made their product, the law assumes they have such expert knowledge.

Business had been booming at my firm for a while. I hadn't been making big money for that long, but it had been long enough to know that despite the potentially massive out of pocket costs my firm would incur, I couldn't think of letting this family walk out of another lawyer's office without at least looking further at their prospects for success.

Although I still wasn't completely convinced I should take the case, I didn't hesitate to tell the Castillos that I was ready to explore the possibilities. After all, I had access to a medical librarian in Washington, DC, who could easily help me find whatever studies existed on benomyl and Benlate. I was more than willing to call her to see where this would lead. The family had surely been through enough over the past three and a half years. What harm could waiting a few more weeks do? "If I find some science out there—anything that supports this claim—I'm totally in," I said. "Let's see where this goes."

Here's what we uncovered in our search:

DuPont created the product Benlate. The active ingredient in Benlate was benomyl. We discovered that benomyl was tested on pregnant rats at the University of California in 1991. The results were really bad. Forty-three percent of the rats' offspring were born with ocular abnormalities such as having no eyes, blindness, and other related eye conditions. Worse, if the rats were fed a protein-deficient diet—which is common in low-income households such as those of migrant workers—the percentage of ocular issues jumped to 61 percent!

Based on this study and the timing of Donna's exposure, I decided I would take the case. Even though the risks were astronomical, I thought it was worth a shot.

I called the Castillos and asked them to come to my office.

"I won't make any promises," I told them, "but if we win, my fee will be a percentage of the money the jury awards you so I'll be able to make a fee and recoup my costs. If we don't win, I'll get no fee at all and won't recover my costs. This pursuit isn't going to cost you a thing. How does that sound?" I asked.

Donna couldn't contain her emotion. She broke down and began to cry again. But this time, they were tears of joy. At least I hoped so. She thanked me over and over again, because not only did someone finally hear her, someone was also finally willing to undertake the fight and fearlessly lead the family through the darkness. I wanted Donna and Juan to know I was in their corner and would act as their advocate for as long as it took to bring DuPont to justice.

As righteous as that may sound, I meant it.

Sometimes you have to look at more than the bottom line. The thing is, in law, as in any profession, you want to do your best to make a difference. At least I do. My father had a need to help people who were down on their luck, whether it involved giving a meal to a homeless man on the street or lending a caring hand to someone who just needed it. Although he could be very tough and demanding, he also had a very big heart. Because he grew up without very much, he knew what it was like to go without or have needs that couldn't be fulfilled. Seeing my dad's charitable ways greatly influenced me to act the same way. I share his need to help others, especially those who are less fortunate or who simply can't do what I can do or have what I have.

In life, when you're generous with your resources, whether money or time, you eventually learn that you're not really giving it away, because you always get it back one way or another. It's that old saying: "What goes around comes around." A lot of people choose a career for the money, but there are those who also want to add value to others' lives. They want to be legends, to build a legacy to be proud of, to effect change in the system, and to make good things happen all around them. I admired attorneys like Ron Motley, who was a pioneer in asbestos litigation and the catalyst that ultimately brought Big Tobacco to its knees. I greatly respected his willingness to take on a cause regardless of potentially insurmountable odds. I am inspired by people like Ron, whose purpose was to take down the three-headed monsters—like the "Big Three" tobacco companies—of the world. I strive to be that type of person every day. Some days I may fall short, but on most days, my aim is true.

I said good-bye to Donna and once again reassured her that everything was going to be okay. Later that night, when I looked into my sons' eyes, I got all the confirmation I needed. There was no doubt about it—I'd made the right decision to help the Castillos. After I shared the story about Daddy's new case and the little boy who was born with no eyes, my youngest son, Andrew, looked up at me and asked, "What do you mean he has no eyes?"

I could tell he was confused by the notion.

"How could something like that happen?" My older son, James, asked with equal wonderment.

I told them both not to worry. I explained in no uncertain terms that Daddy was going after the bad company that sold the dangerous chemicals that caused this boy's mother to get very sick while she was pregnant—so sick that when the baby was born, he had no eyes.

"Wow. I'm so lucky that didn't happen to my mommy," one of the boys said.

Amen to that.

# 2

"You're in America now; you have to speak English."

When my great-grandparents immigrated to the United States from Italy in 1910, they mandated that they and everyone else in the family assimilate. True to this philosophy, when my grandfather was born two years later in Connecticut, his parents rarely spoke their native language around him or their other children. As a result, my father learned only a few Italian words here and there. My great-grandparents believed that to effectively assimilate in America you had to speak only English. That was unfortunate, because it meant I never learned a second language, though I wish I had.

My grandfather worked as a landscaper in Greenwich, Connecticut, where many of his clients lived in large, beautiful old estates. He never made more than twenty dollars a day in his life. He knew the challenges of living hand-to-mouth and desperately wanted a better life for his son. He looked around at the homes where he labored and realized that the only way to get ahead in this new world was through education. For as long as I can remember, my father made it a point to instill in me both his strong work ethic and his belief in the value of education.

Because my grandfather was both hardworking and frugal, he managed to save money so my dad could someday go to college and make something of himself. And that's exactly what my dad did. My father was the first college graduate in our family. He met my mother in high school and married his sweetheart right after he graduated college and ten months later, along came me. His first job after college was in management with AT&T, working in New York City. He spent five years there before becoming a communications consultant specializing in advising corporations on cost-effective telecommunication systems.

A year after AT&T was directed by the federal government to allow competitors to interconnect into public telephone lines, my father started his own company called United Telephone Consulting, which offered the public long-distance service for less than half the price AT&T was charging. Unfortunately, this service was so new consumers were reluctant to leave AT&T as their long distance provider out of fear that their telephone service would somehow be impacted—or worse, turned off—so the company failed. Ultimately, AT&T was sued on anti-trust grounds in 1974. His idea was ahead of its time, but it paved the way for companies such as Sprint to launch their ventures a few years later and become multibillion dollar entities in the process. My dad's vision was spot-on, but his timing wasn't quite right. After his company went under, he spent the rest of his career as a consultant in the industry.

I was around fifteen years old when my dad's company closed. To this day, it makes me sad to think about it. He tried so hard to make the business a success, but he brought his idea to market too early. I know it hurt him deeply, and I can never forget that. It just didn't seem fair. In addition to sadness, I had a sort of anger, which I think subconsciously fueled a drive or ambition in me to seek vindication for my dad.

I am the oldest of my parent's three children, and despite his valiant attempts, for whatever reason, I didn't instinctively embrace his beliefs—at least, not when I was younger. Report card day was always terrifying for me. Although I brought home only two Ds in my life, I've never forgotten the fallout. The first time it happened, I was in the second grade, and the D was for "conduct." Conduct isn't even a class; it's a behavior. That should tell you a little bit about me. You see, I was a renegade, more interested in having a good time than learning.

I got my second D many years later. I was a freshman in high school and was studying Spanish. At the time, I wasn't interested in learning a second language. I guess I felt fully "assimilated." Today's immigrants, however, have a better philosophy: many of them choose not to abandon their roots. They tend to retain their native tongue and cultural habits, which I think is a better way to live. It never made sense to me when people chose to give up their familial history instead of embracing it. I wished my immigrant ancestors had passed along their language and lifestyle to me in addition to the American ways they adopted.

My dad was extremely tough on his children, yet he was also very protective of us, too. His industrious nature was admirable, but for a young boy it was frustrating, because he'd make me spend my entire weekends doing chores around the house and yard instead of playing with my friends. He had me raking leaves, washing the car, and doing anything else he could think of to keep me busy. Whenever I finished a given task, I would look at him with great pride. I was happy to be done with it and always believed that I did a pretty good job. But he rarely agreed.

"Go back and do it over," he'd say.

My mother was the calming force in our family who helped me keep my sanity and avoid any type of meltdown whenever I felt frustrated by this.

My dad wasn't the kind of man to dole out accolades—ever. His father didn't give praise easily, and therefore neither did mine. "Good job" or "Atta boy" weren't part of his vernacular.

At Greenwich High School, I was the second-leading tackler on the football team. We were undefeated—one of three teams in the one-hundred-plus year history of the school to accomplish that feat. While my dad would attend all my games, he was never able to utter "Great game, son" afterward.

He just expected me to excel—to get out there and always do my best.

I didn't realize it at the time, but his high expectations helped me focus on becoming the best I could be at anything I took on. This lack of praise was actually a gift I would learn to appreciate later in life. Ironically, I would discover years later that this man who rarely gave me compliments directly had plenty to say about me to everyone else. Over time, I would hear story after story from friends and even mere acquaintances about how well my dad thought I was doing on the football field, in school, with charities, in my career, as a father, and so on and so forth. It was clear to them that he was as proud as a father could be.

By the time I was in my teens, I worked during summers and holidays for my grandfather as his assistant landscaper. I can't remember a summer when I didn't have a job. My father put all the money I earned in the bank and wouldn't let me touch it. I didn't understand his logic then, but I certainly do now.

My dad's parents divorced when he was only ten years old. My grandmother took my dad's nine-year-old sister and my grandfather took my dad. They split the children as though they were nothing more than property. Sadly, my father didn't see his mother again for forty years. From the time Dad was ten years old through high school, his four aunts took on the role of "mother," each of them feeding him dinner on different days of the week. They were very nice ladies, but they also had their own children, and my dad naturally felt like a bit of an outcast or a burden to them.

Because of his childhood, my dad was very protective of his family and insisted on always knowing where his kids were at all times and doing whatever he could to shield us from harm. As a matter of practice, he kept all of us close, sometimes to the point of being downright stifling—especially as I entered my teenage years.

As a teen, I'd sometimes sneak away at night and go to parties or do whatever I could to break free of the boundaries and rules he set up—rules that I was expected to strictly abide by. After I graduated from high school in 1975, I moved to Santa Barbara, California, without any warning to or discussion with my family. I wanted to be with my girlfriend, who had relocated there with her mother. I lived with them and got a job caddying at a local country club. I was madly in love, or so I thought.

Hell, I was eighteen years old. What did I know about *love*?

Three weeks later, after stressing out about my future, I found myself back home. I realized that if I didn't start college in the fall, I'd never get a degree. My father had always promised he'd pay for my education, but said many times over the years that everything else was on me. By the time I started school, I had nearly ten thousand dollars saved, all because of my dad's forethought and planning. That was a lot of money back in the mid 1970s. Though my dad didn't give me access to the money, I always knew it was there for a rainy day.

By the time I was ready to attend to college, only one thought was driving my decision as to where I should go: "The farther away, the better!" My dad wanted me to stay close to home and attend a school that was in or near New England, such as Bucknell. That wasn't where I saw myself at all. So I went south. I started at the University of Miami in the fall of 1975. For a brief time I thought about applying to the Air Force Academy. I loved flying, and though I hadn't ever sat in a pilot's seat before, I was certain it would be thrilling. However, Miami seemed like it would be a lot more fun. I didn't even visit the campus. Nope—I applied based solely on the beautiful brochure. The pictures made the school look as though it were located directly on the ocean, which I would soon discover wasn't the case. What appeared to be the sea was actually a lake.

I still fondly recall the many vacations my family took to Miami when I was a young boy. Sometimes we'd go by train from Connecticut. It would take twenty-four hours to navigate along the Eastern Seaboard. Other times, we flew or drove. One thing I remembered from those family excursions was how nice the weather was all the time. When I weighed New England against Miami, the warmer climate won hands down. Miami was definitely the place to be.

One thing I knew for sure was that I desperately wanted my freedom and the ability to spread my wings. If I stayed close to home, I didn't believe I could do that. I love my dad with all my heart and certainly wouldn't be the person I am today if it wasn't for his strict ways, but I also understood that I needed to be on my own to figure out who I was as a young man entering the real world for the first time. Aside from education, I suppose independence and the opportunity for self-discovery are two of the greatest gifts college provides.

I already knew my roommate, Scott McConnell, because he was from Greenwich. We were in the first grade together and had stayed friends throughout the years. It was comforting to have someone from home around as we both made our way through our freshman year. Scott's dad gave him forty dollars a month for spending money. Because I was the first kid my father ever sent to college, he had no idea that giving me spending money was the right thing to do, let alone how much was a good amount. It wasn't until he spoke with Scott's dad that I started getting forty dollars a month, too, which still made us the poorest guys on our floor of the dorm. Everyone else had their parents' credit cards and endlessly deep pockets, and they all drove the latest-model sports cars.

We didn't like being the guys with no money, so we came up with a plan to pool our monthly stipend, buy eighty dollars' worth of alcohol, and sell drinks out of our room. By charging fifty cents a cocktail, we turned our eighty-dollar investment into seven hundred dollars! Our underground speakeasy was a glorious moneymaker until the university shut us down for being in violation of school rules.

My first two years of college were wild. I joined a fraternity and spent most of my time drinking, partying, and chasing beautiful girls. I also played football as a walk-on for two years. I wasn't the biggest guy, but I was a fearless one-hundred-eighty-eight-pound scrapper. After practice I'd go drinking with my buddies. I was small but tough. One thing was for certain—I was trained not to take shit from anyone, not even Fresco, a badass, drug-dealing punk who lived on our dorm floor freshman year. He was a fifth-degree black belt who used to terrorize everybody on the floor. All the guys were afraid of him—except, of course, me.

On a late October night, after having more than a few drinks, I was waiting for a girl I'd invited back to my room for a pizza date to arrive. I was wearing my favorite canary-yellow pants, a white T-shirt, and loafers with no socks. I was pacing back and forth. This was no ordinary girl. She was a prim, proper, homecoming-queen type of girl. She was so hot that my roommate couldn't believe she had agreed to come back to our dorm. To be honest, neither could I.

I left the door to the room open so she could walk right in. Instead, while I was waiting, Fresco barged in, grabbed a slice of pizza, and shoved it into his mouth.

"Did I say you could have that?" I asked. I was pissed.

Fresco looked at me, paused, and then took another bite without uttering a word.

That's when I pushed him into the hallway.

We started brawling as though our lives depended on it.

The walls of the dorm were made of thick cinder blocks that were painted beige. We punched, kicked, and threw each other against those walls for nearly fifteen minutes. This was a battle to the end. I wasn't trying to win; I was trying to kill him, and he was trying to do the same to me.

The other guys in the dorm didn't even attempt to break up the fight. Instead, they drank beer and watched us beat the shit out of each other.

My strategy was to stay close to Fresco, because I knew he'd kick my ass if I didn't. Suddenly, and quite unexpectedly, he jumped up into the air and kicked me in the head as hard as he could. This was, hands down, the best move in his arsenal. Too bad, really, because his foot connected with my head in an area that had no feeling from getting hit all the time in football. His kick threw me back a couple of feet, but it didn't knock me out. I stayed up and managed to charge at him with everything I had. I was banging his head against the corner of the wall when someone shouted that the campus police were coming.

I had one hand clenched around his throat and the other on his forehead when I gave him one final push and walked away. There was blood splattered everywhere. His and mine. It was a pretty nasty scene.

When it was over, my shirt was torn, my pants were covered in blood and dirt, and my hair looked like Jack Nicholson's in *One Flew Over the Cuckoo's Nest*. I looked like a butcher after a twelve-hour day at the slaughterhouse. I went back to my room and tried to straighten out my appearance, as if it would make a difference. When I turned around, the girl I was waiting for was suddenly in the doorway.

"What happened?" she asked.

"I had a little problem with the pizza delivery. But it's all fine now," I said, handing her a slice.

She took one little bite and suddenly remembered a test she needed to study for. She was gone before I could say another word.

I had a lot of anger when I first arrived in Miami, but I never physically fought with anyone again after that night with Fresco. I didn't like the way it made me feel. My dad used to snap like that; every year around the holidays he'd become intolerable and just lose his cool. He wanted everything to be perfect, but the reality is life doesn't work that way. Whenever something went wrong, his temper would flair. It's not that he didn't love his family—he did. Perhaps to a fault. It was just very painful for him around Christmastime knowing that his mom was out there somewhere, but not with him.

My father did his best to appear happy, but inside he was hurting. Sadly, he spent many years living that way, until, four decades after they last saw each other, he and his mother finally reunited. It was in 1985. My father was at a carnival in a neighboring town with my mom and another couple, his friend Joe Longo and his wife. While they were all having a good time, Joe suddenly turned to my dad and said, "Hey, Lou, I think that's your mom over there."

Sure enough, it was. The two made eye contact and immediately ran toward each other. They embraced for several minutes and broke down in tears. Until this reunion, I had had no idea that my grandmother was alive. My father never spoke of her except to tell us the story of his parents' separation when he was ten years old.

I met my grandmother for the first time at her home in Stamford, Connecticut, around Thanksgiving. She told me that her only wish during their forty years apart had been to see my father once again. After that fateful night, they saw each other every single day for lunch or dinner until she died five and a half months later.

# 3

I WAS PRIMARILY drawn to the Castillo case because of the massive challenge it presented. Once again, I was confronting the bully. The thought of slaying the dragon—which is how I referred to DuPont at the time—was really appealing to me. From a career point of view, if we prevailed, it would surely be my biggest and greatest conquest. This drive to win, as you now know, was cultivated in me by my father, who always demanded more from me than even I knew I had inside. But the idea of winning wasn't the only thing motivating me. Making a difference in the lives of people who had possibly been impacted by the chemical Benlate was big.

I had already made a difference in lots of people's lives before this opportunity came knocking. The asbestos cases I'd tried in the past allowed so many people and their families to live comfortably for the rest of their lives, even though many of those lives were already limited by the time we went to trial. Winning the case was their last hope. That's a heavy load to carry on one's shoulders, but I didn't mind. It was worth it if I could, in some small way, make my clients' lives and deaths easier.

Several years before the Castillo case, I represented a client named Vinny Casasanta in an asbestos case. Vinny was a super nice guy—one of the nicest people I've ever known. When we met, he was fifty-one years old and dying from mesothelioma. The first time Vinny and his wife came from their home in Connecticut to see me, they stayed at the Fontainebleau, the same hotel they had honeymooned in many years before. Their trip was emotional for a variety of reasons, but mostly because this would be their last hurrah, and they knew it.

Throughout his career, Vinny had worked with a toxic fireproofing spray made by W. R. Grace, a high-performance specialty chemical manufacturing company. That was our target. It was the early 1990s. I was seeking at least a $10 million verdict against the company, and at the time, I believed we had a very good chance of winning.

The case was set to begin on a Monday. The Friday morning prior, we received an offer to settle for a little over $1 million. When I initially shared the offer with Vinny, he had absolutely no interest in accepting what I considered to be a paltry amount. He also worried that there wasn't enough money in the settlement for me. I assured him that he should not be concerned about me—I had lots of other cases, and the decision had to be his. I firmly believed we had a very good chance of getting at least $10 million. I didn't think Vinny would settle. I felt he'd go all the way. I was fired up to win for him and it would have been a very big verdict.

I liked Vinny from the start. He was a hell of a nice man, and someone I still think of as a dream client for many reasons. It appeared as though we were on the same page until my phone rang two hours later. It was Vinny. He and his wife had talked it over and decided to settle for the million-plus dollars that was on the table. He talked about the little addition he wanted to build on their house and then told me all about their grandchildren. After discussing it with his wife, he said he could rest a lot easier knowing the money would keep her comfortable for the rest of her life.

"I know I won't be around to do that, Jim," he solemnly said.

When I heard that, I knew we were done. I didn't even try to talk him out of his decision or sway him the other way.

I called the attorneys for W. R. Grace and told them there would be no trial—the case was over. They knew they got off easy, and so did I. I sat alone in my office feeling very down, because at the time I thought this was a dream case for me and now it wasn't going to happen.

I was absorbed in my own self pity and vanity.

A few hours later, my phone rang again. It was Vinny. He was crying this time.

Before I could ask if he had changed his mind, he told me what a difference I'd made in their lives. The money would change everything for them during the limited time he had left.

"I'm at peace, Jim," he said.

And in my heart and soul, I could feel that he was.

It was that exact moment when I realized how wrong I'd been in my assessment of this case. It wasn't about me. It was about Vinny and his family. Giving them peace was exactly what my job is all about.

Each case I take is someone else's dispute. It's my temporary battle to fight on their behalf, but in the end, it's their quarrel—not mine. It's their monkey, their circus. I am merely the ringleader.

A massive verdict is more about ego than anything else. My job is to get the best possible results for my clients. It's about their happiness. Not my vanity.

That's it. Nothing more; nothing less.

Getting that last call from Vinny gave me more satisfaction than being awarded a large sum of money on their behalf ever would have. I get a high from helping people. You could say it's my drug of choice. There's no better or more infectious feeling than knowing people are happy because you helped them out of their crisis. This case greatly influenced my way of thinking and how I moved forward in my career.

And what a roller coaster it has been.

# 4

BY MY JUNIOR year of college, the realization that I ought to get serious with my life began to set in. It's safe to say that going to class and keeping up with my schoolwork had been a low priority for the first two years. While I was able to maintain a high-enough grade point average, I was hardly living up to my potential. If I got a B, it was the lowest B possible. It was the same for every A and C I got too.

At the time, I wanted to become an accountant, but I knew that partying, pulling average grades, and just skating by weren't going to get me there. I've always been the kind of guy who waits until the last minute to get things done and who works best under intense pressure. In fact, it's almost as though I need a hard deadline breathing down my neck, forcing me to keep pace. When a target date isn't set, I'll create one as a self-imposed hurdle I have to jump in order to accomplish my goal. If I know there's a bona fide reason, I will work like a maniac, driving myself until I complete the race—but usually I finish by the skin of my teeth. It's this challenge to beat the clock that creates momentum for me. Without it, I'll just procrastinate.

As the sand fell through the hourglass, I stopped and assessed my future. I didn't want to mess up the rest of my life by screwing up in college. But by the time I had this epiphany, I had only a short while to get my grade point average up—especially since I wanted to become a Certified Public Accountant (CPA) and go on to get my master's degree. CPAs must meet the highest standards in education, experience, and ethics. It is the strict adherence to these standards that maintains the necessary skill set and helps formulate trust and confidence between CPAs and their clients. I was now officially in success mode studying day in and day out.

One hot, humid night, some friends and I were at Baskin-Robbins getting a mint-chocolate-chip ice cream sundae. This had become a ritual of ours. We usually went late after a night of partying. I swear, sometimes the taste of those sundaes was better than an orgasm. Just as we were about to leave the store, we ran into Alan LaBell, the president of the student government. I knew Alan because he lived in the fraternity house next to mine. We struck up a conversation, and while we were talking he asked me if I'd consider being on the Student Supreme Court.

"Yeah, sure. What exactly is it?" I asked. I had no idea what he was talking about, but something about the idea intrigued me.

Alan told me to meet him the following Monday at the student union, where he would appoint me to the court.

When I arrived, there was a group of eight kids who all appeared to be very serious. I could tell they were excellent students who cared about academics—maybe a little more than I was comfortable with—and yet if I wanted to change my direction, I sensed that this was the perfect place for me to be. I stood frozen for a moment because I could tell they were wondering, *Who is this aberration who just walked through the door? How the hell did he get here?* It was obvious that someone in the group was not like all the others. I was the odd man out.

I scanned the room, looking for the friendliest face I could find. There were two women on the court, so I sat next to the one I thought was the prettiest.

Her name was Diane. She was very attractive and bright. From the moment I laid eyes on her, I wanted to ask her out, but she didn't seem like the kind of girl you take to the Rathskeller to drink a pitcher of beer. At the time, that was about all I could afford. I didn't have the means to wine and dine a gorgeous girl. But thankfully that didn't matter.

Diane and I immediately hit it off and quickly became inseparable. We spent our days and nights studying and working hard together. We married two years later, in June of 1980. I was twenty-three years old, and, true to the goal I had set for myself, I was working as a CPA with a master's degree at one of the "Big Eight" accounting firms. However, I soon realized accounting wasn't the career I wanted and decided to go to law school. Four months into the marriage, I started attending law school at the University of Miami in the evenings. I had no choice but to attend the evening program because I had to continue working as an accountant to pay the bills.

It wasn't until I started working full-time and attending law school at night that I realized how easily I can become bored when I am not engaged and totally focused on something. Looking back, I recognized that my undergrad studies didn't hold my attention because the pace was too slow for me. There were too many distractions that held my interest more than those classes did. However, now that I was more focused than I'd ever been before, I had no free time for anything else. My life outside of work and school was nearly nonexistent. This, of course, wasn't the ideal way to start a marriage. I never had enough time to nurture my new relationship, let alone enjoy the so-called honeymoon period.

It turns out that my mind works in a very linear and logical way— two great traits for a budding attorney. I typically see things in lists and have the ability to parse out each point so I can analyze it better.

It didn't matter whether I was writing appellate briefs on the statute of frauds, punitive damages, or the exclusion of a witness; I'd always look at each issue and easily decide how I wanted to organize and dissect it before moving on. Before I knew it, and with very little effort, I'd have the whole skeleton of an argument in front of me to talk through and refine. It may not be a perfect system, but it works for me.

I spent 1981 and 1982 working fifty-five hours a week as an accountant while also completing my first two years of law school. During the fall semesters of those first two years I would take off only Thanksgiving and Christmas day. My spring semesters were no better. I used to spend endless hours dreaming about my third year, when I hoped and believed I could just be a "normal" student and clerk fifteen hours a week at a law firm somewhere in Miami.

It didn't turn out quite that way. The third year of law school was anything but a dream.

I interviewed for a coveted clerk's position in the tax department at Greenberg Traurig, a top-tier firm that now has offices all over the world. At the end of the interview, the hiring partner said, "We'll get back to you within a week."

"So far so good," I thought as I left their office, believing I had nailed it.

The very next day, while I was on campus, I crossed paths with Dr. Charlie Calhoun, the chairman of the accounting program. While I was in graduate school I was in charge of the accounting clinic that helped students understand complicated concepts they might have had difficulty grasping. Charlie said, "Jim, I was about to give you a call."

"Oh yeah? About what?"

"I have a position for you in the accounting department," he said.

"What type of position?"

"Teaching two cost-accounting classes every morning at 8:00 a.m. for $1,500 per class, per semester. What do you think?" Dr. Calhoun was genuinely excited to present this opportunity to me, which of course made me feel really good.

"Sounds great. I'll take it!" I said without thinking.

Wait a minute, what about the clerking position I just applied for? What if I got that, too? How could I ever take on so much at once?

Naturally, the very next day I got a call from the hiring partner at Greenberg Traurig offering me the clerking job. As the type of guy who not only likes to ride in overdrive but also excels at it, I accepted that position as well. In my overzealousness, I created a schedule that was just as jam-packed, if not more so, as my first two years of law school. I had just committed to taking eighteen credits a semester, clerking fifteen hours a week, and teaching accounting to eighty students every morning at 8:00 a.m.

Yeah, it was a grind, but it was worth it. Some very good and some bad (depending on how you look at them) developments came out of that overwhelming third year of law school.

Quite unexpectedly, my teaching position led me to start a side business representing professional football players. I know it seems out of the blue, but one of my students was Keith Griffin, the brother of Archie Griffin, who was the only two-time Heisman Trophy winner ever. Keith enjoyed my class very much, and knew I was also in law school. One day, he approached me to talk about his future. "Hey, Jim, are you going to be representing football players when you graduate from law school?"

"Yes, I definitely plan on doing that," I said, even though at the time I hadn't even thought about a career in sports management. Once Keith put the idea in my head, I realized that it was a pretty good one, so I immediately jumped at the opportunity. As it turned out, I never represented Keith, but a year later, I did end up representing a player by the name of Albert Bentley, who was a star on the first national championship team at the University of Miami and a top draft pick with the Michigan Panthers of the now defunct USFL (United States Football League). That, in turn, prompted me to sign quite a few other top players over the next several years, including Eddie Brown (the 1985 NFL Rookie of the Year), James Brooks (a star at Auburn), Tim

McGee (a star at Tennessee), and Ickey Woods (creator of the "Ickey Shuffle").

As a result of my excessive schedule and commitments, I was completely stressed out. The first three years of my marriage were consumed by work. I'd become very absorbed in my career and in my determination to get ahead. I was making difficult sacrifices at home in order to provide a good life for Diane and me. The downside was that I often felt as though I was living in a coma because I was studying and working so much. Although my academic and professional accomplishments were growing, I wasn't developing at all on a personal level. I didn't even have time to think about my relationship with Diane, let alone time to realize what a toll my perpetual absence was taking on both of us. Having grown up in a frugal household, I understood the value of money and the incredible amount of hard work, commitment, and perseverance it takes to earn it. No one in my family had ever pursued a professional career, let alone graduated from law school. I created the path on which I was walking to honor my family.

My hard work really paid off, because I earned straight As in my final semester of undergraduate schooling and throughout graduate school as well. When I finally got my law degree in 1983, my top-tier grades, combined with my experience as a CPA, put me in a prime position to seek work in the biggest markets—and to me, there was no bigger market than New York. However, I was a total novice at the application process.

I applied to several top firms in Manhattan and was rejected by all of them. They were only looking at Ivy League graduates. If you didn't go to Yale or Harvard, you couldn't even get in the door for an interview.

I had no clue how stiff the competition would be for those jobs. I wasn't from a pedigreed family with connections, nor did I really know where I should apply. From my point of view, I was just as good as any Ivy Leaguer. I learned everything I knew about the law from the exact same textbooks those guys studied. I didn't think their profes-

sors taught the subject any better than mine, yet I was still sent packing without ever being given the chance to prove myself. It seemed
like an unfair barometer of who was good and who was not. I would
eventually go up against these lawyers in the courtroom on a day-
to-day basis anyway, which is where the true test takes place. Even
though I knew I could compete with these players, I wasn't allowed
to get in the game. It felt a lot like making a team and being forced to
sit on the bench when you know you're just as good as—if not better
than—anyone else on the field. I had no choice except to get out there
and prove myself.

By the time I realized it would be better to stay in Miami, it was
spring, and too late to be taken seriously by any of the big firms there.
Their new hires had been brought on six months earlier, sometime
in the fall. In the end, there were no solid job opportunities for me,
which meant that I was flat-out unemployed, with zero prospects on
the horizon. I was studying for the bar exam with no job in sight.

I began to feel very depressed by my plight. I had worked my ass off
day and night to conquer the world, and the world wasn't responding.
All those years of dedication suddenly felt incredibly useless.

Thankfully, my wife, who had graduated from law school a year
before me, was working and bringing home enough money to cover
our bills while I studied for the bar exam and continued to look for a
job. We were living in a humble condominium in West Kendall. We
had very little overhead, so neither of us worried much about how we
would make ends meet. Although it wasn't an easy time, we both knew
that someday I'd land a job. I started to really think about my whole
"conquer the world" philosophy. Who am I? What is my purpose?
Why am I here?

Then came what I consider to be one of the seminal moments in
my life.

One afternoon during a break from studying, I took a walk to get
some ice cream, as I often did. It was a stiflingly hot and humid day,
typical of South Florida in the summer. I found these study breaks

to be good for my head. I usually spent the time contemplating my future. On this particular day, I watched a plumber's van whiz past me. I looked at the truck and the man behind the wheel and thought to myself, "He's got it all figured out." He was probably making three hundred dollars a week, had a family he went home to at night, a small mortgage he could pay, and no stress about where his next dollar was coming from. His life was stable and settled. That kind of life suddenly seemed very appealing to me.

I took a bite of my fast-melting mint-chocolate-chip ice cream and realized I didn't need to have a big life. Who really does? I certainly hadn't grown up with great luxury, so why was I aiming for that now? A less-is-more lifestyle was actually ideal. That's what living is really about.

In any event, as soon as I let go of my overreaching mind-set, everything seemed to fall into place. I passed the bar exam and was immediately offered three jobs: the first was with the state attorney's office, the second with a small local law firm, and the third with a well-known medium-sized defense firm with a solid reputation in downtown Miami. I accepted the position with the medium-sized firm, Kimbrell & Hamann, where I quickly found a niche as a trial lawyer and representing professional athletes.

After I started work, I finally had the freedom to experience who my wife was and who I was at the time. It was 1984, and I was happier than I'd been in years. I didn't have school at night anymore, so every day felt like a vacation. Up until then, I could take Diane out only on Friday nights—and even then we would spend only a couple of hours together before I had to go back to studying. Now we were able to go out on a Tuesday at 6:30 if we wanted to, without any restrictions.

As it turned out, my time at Kimbrell & Hamann was short-lived. This medium-sized insurance defense firm was made up of a very good and conservative group of lawyers. Unfortunately, I had trouble defending insurance companies that I thought were taking unnecessary advantage of poor and helpless individuals. As a result of my strong feelings, I didn't think I was a good fit. Within a year, I accepted an associate position at the large, prestigious firm of Finley Kumble, where I hoped I could grow my business. However, I ran into challenges there, too. I soon learned that many of the young partners wanted to get involved in my sports practice. I brought a lot to the table, but none of the partners would allow me to operate on my own as a mere associate. I had negotiated my autonomy with the partner who hired me, explaining that the sports business required more of a one-on-one relationship. But it didn't work out that way, so I decided to start my own trial law firm and sports management company. I had saved barely enough money to pull it off, but fortunately I had enough of a client base to draw from to at least launch the business. I knew things would be tough at first and would require a lot of patience, but I was up to the task.

On May 13, 1985, I hired a secretary and opened my small office in Miami. I paid her twenty-five thousand dollars a year and took home the same amount myself. I was representing athletes and trying cases, doing everything I could to build a practice. This new venture wasn't helping my marital issues much, especially because I wasn't around a lot and wasn't bringing home enough money to make up for my obvious absence.

During my second year in business, one of my clients was busted for possessing cocaine and an unlicensed handgun. He was a young, high-profile football player, so this became headline news. All the negative publicity it created prevented me from signing any new players that year. They were all afraid of being associated with me or that client. The lack of new business put a tremendous financial strain on the firm, nearly causing me to shut my doors for good. To stay alive and make payroll, I maxed out my one and only credit card for $5,000 and borrowed $5,000 from my old buddy Hercules. My wife was constantly telling me I should close down the practice and go work for a big law firm instead. This advice both angered and depressed me.

While my firm was going through this rough patch in 1987, one of my professional football clients was Eddie Brown. He had been named the 1985 NFL Rookie of the Year and was making a million six for four years. At the time, I thought that was outlandish money. In contrast, I wasn't even taking home a paycheck so I could help keep my law firm alive.

Then came what I now see as the ultimate defining moment of my life—that moment when you make a decision that affects who you are from that point on.

One day out of nowhere, I received a refund check in the mail from State Farm in the amount of $3,000. Eddie Brown had changed insurance companies and asked me to handle the transaction. Although the check was meant for him, it came to me with my name on it. At the time, I was so desperate for money that I very seriously contemplated depositing it into my account. I was financially at rock bottom. There wasn't a chance Eddie would ever know what I had done. I thought long and hard about how badly I needed that money, and naturally assured myself I'd pay it back to him someday. I had the check in my sweaty hand, literally staring at it for several minutes. Then it became clear.

"Fuck it," I said. "You can't do that. You're better than this."

I picked up the phone, called Eddie, and told him about the check.

"Just put it in my account, man," he said, cool as could be.

And that's exactly what I did.

There are times in your life when what appears to be a simple solution creates far bigger problems for you in the long run. My back was against the wall, and there's no doubt my morals and character were being tested. Here's what I know for sure: you can never go wrong doing the right thing. As desperate as I was, I would never have been able to live with the decision I was pondering that day if I had gone through with it. I had to operate by a set of standards that guided me in everything I did, or someday I'd pay the price for my lack of judgment.

I wasn't a scammer or a thief. I was a decent, hardworking attorney just trying to make it on my own. Being broke was better than having no soul.

I believe in karma.

By the end of 1988, things were finally on the upswing. I was making around seventy thousand dollars a year, which I considered a lot of money at the time. Now, less than two short years after my ultimate defining moment with that $3,000 insurance check, life was about to radically change for me. Here's what happened.

In early December 1988, I attended a judicial fund-raiser for a then state court judge—now a federal judge—named Ursula Ungaro. At the event, I was pulled aside by David Wells, who was a young partner at Greenberg Traurig, where I had clerked during my last year of law school. He told me he had given my name to a guy named Pete Angelos, who was looking for a young, ambitious trial lawyer to represent asbestos victims in Florida.

Before coming to me, Pete had worked with three other firms to handle twenty-one asbestos cases in Florida from 1985 to 1988. None of the firms had had any success with these cases. Now Pete was looking for help again. I was the lucky one.

I learned that most of the lawyers handling asbestos cases were affiliated with established firms that specialized in this area. I wasn't one of those guys. But the numbers looked potentially very good. So I met with Pete in Baltimore and agreed to take over the cases. Despite the fact that I had no help and no mentor, I quickly made a name for myself and reaped the rewards for those efforts.

The first case I tried was in 1991 representing a man named Joe Zabka. Joe was a pipefitter and was dying from lung cancer, a condition he developed as a result of smoking and working with a pipe-covering product manufactured by Owens Corning.

I drove to Joe's house in Hollywood, Florida, where I met with him and his wife of forty-eight years. He was a very nice and decent working-class guy who was in a union in the neighboring city of Fort

Lauderdale. Joe was living on oxygen and was barely able to walk. He was in pretty bad shape. I liked the guy and felt bad for his situation, so I said I'd take his case to trial.

When I met Joe for the first time, I had no idea that no one else was trying lung cancer cases caused by asbestos because of the tobacco defense. This defense is based on the premise that smokers are much more likely to develop lung cancer from their smoking than from other factors, such as working with asbestos.

Perhaps it was my inexperience in this area, but I wasn't deterred. I happen to believe that being naïve isn't such a bad thing—it simply means that you're the type of person who tends to reject the conventional wisdom that something is a problem. I also knew that a 1985 Surgeon General's report showed a synergy between smoke and asbestos. According to this report, if you work with asbestos but don't smoke, you're five times more likely to develop lung cancer than someone who doesn't smoke and doesn't work with asbestos. If you don't work with asbestos but do smoke, you're ten times more likely to get lung cancer. If you both work with asbestos and smoke, you're fifty times more likely to develop lung cancer. In other words, a smoker who works with asbestos increases his risk fivefold! Joe made it clear in his video deposition before trial that he didn't want to be compensated for smoking because he chose to do that for pleasure. However, he didn't choose to breathe asbestos for pleasure. Sadly, no one—in particular the defendant, Owens Corning—warned Joe about the dangers of asbestos.

By the time the case went to trial in 1991, Joe had died. He gave a very good video deposition before his death, which we used at trial. We won the case for a little over a million dollars, in large part because we made it clear that Joe's damages should be reduced by twenty percent to account for his smoking. The final payout was $850,000. I believe the jury had a lot of respect for this decision. I won my very first asbestos trial with no assistance from anyone.

After the trial, I received a call from Eric Johnson, the head of the local union. He asked if we could meet for lunch.

"Sure," I said, not realizing the connection.

We met at the City Club, located in my office building. "The reason I wanted to meet you is because Joe Zabka was my best friend," Eric said. "I wanted to personally thank you for taking care of Joe and his family. It means a lot to me and the fellas in the union."

I was stunned yet grateful for his acknowledgment. I had just done my job, but it felt good to hear someone tell me what a good job I did. As we finished our lunch, Eric turned to me and asked, "Can you represent people in other states?"

"Yeah, sure I can. Why?" In actuality, at the time I could file a case in Florida as long as one defendant was located in the state.

"I know the business agent for Local 537 in Boston and another guy in Chicago. If you're interested, I'll set you up with these guys."

"I appreciate the vote of confidence. Thank you, Mr. Johnson."

Within weeks of that lunch, I was hopping on planes and meeting with these guys. They were in charge of their whole unions—thousands of people and potential clients. After we met, they started recommending me as their go-to lawyer, and as a result, 99 percent of their cases came my way. Eighteen months later, I had gone from representing one hundred people to representing *four thousand*. Before I knew it, I was making serious money, and realized I would never have to worry about my income again. I had gone from the outhouse to the palace overnight.

"You're one lucky son of bitch," I thought. Not only was I doing good for other people, I was also reaping the rewards—big-time.

Life was good.

# 5

There are three rules I live by in life.

The first is "There's nothing wrong with having fun."

The second is "Try not to hurt others."

And the third is "Help as many people as you can."

To me, the third is the real scorecard of my time here on earth.

Whenever I think about the day I'll finally meet my Maker, I wonder whether I will be leaving the world a better place because of my contributions. If the answer is that the world is the same or worse as when I entered it, well, then I didn't do enough. At least, not by how I measure things. Then there is the karma.

If I had cashed that $3,000 check from State Farm, there's no way I would have achieved what came my way after that ultimate defining moment. In many ways, I believe the karma earned by deciding not to cash my client's check is what gave me the financial wherewithal to later take on the Castillo case. Without those good years in between, I wouldn't have been able to sustain the costs of such a big case. Moments like that one test your mettle and force you to decide who you are going to be.

The same thing happened the moment I chose to take on the Castillos' fight.

By the time I took the family's case, I was making more money than I needed. Giving back had become extremely important to me. Anyone can write a check when they have the money in the bank to cover it, but giving your time, energy, and attention requires a different type of commitment. I understood that this type of case would be costly in both money *and* time.

As a way of covering or hedging our bet, the firm also took on the cases of the twenty-nine Scottish families in the MACS support group for a future fight against DuPont, because we knew the chances of winning the Castillos' case in the first trial of its kind were, realistically speaking, remote. Taking on the additional families meant even more time and money would be necessary to see this battle through to the bitter end.

At the time, no one had ever won a first-impression toxic tort case, whether it involved asbestos, tobacco, or some other drug or chemical. A first-impression tort case, as the name implies, involves a new cause of action that has never been brought by anyone in any court anywhere. It typically takes many trials before you can taste victory in a new tort claim. For instance, asbestos took ten trials before there was a first win by my friend and legendary trial lawyer Ron Motley, whose work had inspired me for years. Tobacco was even worse, taking more than sixty attempts by multiple attorneys over several decades. In those cases, the evidence and understanding of what it would take to prove the facts got a little better each time. Every new trial represented an opportunity for those pioneering lawyers to find more documents and testimony and hone and refine their arguments, and therefore create and present a stronger case.

Let's face it: it was obvious from the start that the Castillos' case had the potential to lead me into the land of infinity. Because there had never been such a case before, there was no template we could use or improve upon in our fight against DuPont. It had corporate lawyers on the payroll, ready to answer calls day and night. Those attorneys were hired to crush guys like me under mounds of paperwork, document searches, filings, and costs. This left us with no choice but to chart our own course and navigate the treacherous terrain on our own as best as we could. I knew I couldn't let the process go on forever because I had other clients whose needs were equally important, but I was sure there wouldn't be a quick settlement, either. I went into the case knowing that DuPont was counting on us eventually backing down. That's what they plan for. They certainly would try to create as many roadblocks as they possibly could during the discovery process to make this matter go away. To them, we were like an irritating pimple on their ass. To cause them excruciating pain, we would not only have to win on our first try, we'd have to win big. Of course, both of those prospects were unprecedented, and I knew it.

While Donna showed me pictures of her son during our first meeting, it wasn't until the third time I met with the Castillos that I really *saw* the photos of Johnny. He was a cute kid, with blond hair and an infectious smile. He looked totally normal except that his eyelids were closed—and there was nothing behind them. They weren't rounded like my son's lids are when he's sleeping. At the time, only 1 in 10,000 babies worldwide were born with microphthalmia.

In the courtroom, you can use various types of scientific findings to back your claim. Animal studies and human studies are the major types of cited research. The reality, however, is that animal studies aren't always predictive of what the impact will be on a human. What we do know, though, is that the reactions of rats and primates to most chemicals and drugs are closer to human reactions than any other animals' reactions. For instance, a reaction found in a rat will appear in humans 80 percent of the time. Animal studies are significant in cases like the Castillos', and yet when it comes to presenting them as evidence during the trial, they aren't weighed nearly as strongly as they should be. Courts won't allow a case to be built solely on animal studies. Through the years, the courts—and in some places legislatures—have cut back significantly on what is admissible science in the courtroom. The DuPonts of the world have expended enormous sums of money to protect themselves in the courtroom by having a lot of science excluded from the courtroom. On one hand, a company like DuPont will submit these kinds of studies to the EPA to get a product licensed. But when they get sued over the product's safety and the injured party seeks to admit into evidence the same study that the manufacturer presented earlier to the EPA, the study is suddenly called "junk science."

As for human studies, in a chemical exposure case like Donna's, we were severely limited because of the ethical implications of exposing humans to chemicals for testing purposes. The only acceptable human tests in these cases were dermal skin transmission tests and in vitro tests done at the cellular level. Because of the risk, dermal skin transmission tests are performed on human cadaver skin to calculate how much of a chemical travels through the skin.

The bottom line was, we would have to make our case with animal studies, dermal transmission studies, in vitro studies, chemistry, basic anatomy and biology, and finally with something called a differential diagnosis—the ruling out of other possible causes, if any, by process of elimination. It's standard operating procedure in medicine and science.

Once we proved that Benlate could cause microphthalmia, we would have to rule out other possible causes. As part of the differential diagnosis with Donna, we had to consider genetics and other environmental causes besides Benlate, such as an overdose of vitamin K or hyperthermia.

# 6

To BEGIN PREPARING for a trial, both sides engage in what is referred to as discovery. This is the formal process of exchanging information between the opposing parties about the witnesses they will call to the stand and the evidence they plan to present at trial. Discovery enables the parties to determine before the trial begins what evidence they may choose to present. It's designed to prevent trial by ambush, in which one side doesn't learn of the other side's evidence or witnesses until the trial is already under way, leaving no time to obtain counterevidence.

One of the most common methods of discovery is taking depositions. A deposition is out-of-court testimony given under oath by any person involved in the case. It can be used at trial or in preparation for trial. It may be taken in the form of a written transcript, a video, or both. In most states, either of the parties may take the deposition of the other party, or of any witness. Both sides have the right to be present during depositions.

Depositions enable a party to know in advance what a witness will say at trial. Depositions can also be taken to obtain the testimony of important witnesses who can't appear during the trial. In that case, the transcript is read into evidence or the video is played at trial.

Typically a witness's deposition is taken by the opposing side and used not only to discover facts but also to discredit the witness's testimony at trial if the trial testimony is different than the testimony taken during the deposition. Most commonly, expert witnesses are deposed by the opposition to show bias or some sort of monetary interest in the litigation. These witnesses are hired by a party and paid to present their testimony. A lawyer's dream is when inconsistent testimony is uncovered and he or she can ask a witness in front of a jury at trial, "Are you lying now, or were you lying then?"

Depositions usually consist of a direct examination, followed by cross-examination from the other side. In addition to taking depositions, either party may submit written questions, called interrogatories, to the other party, which are answered in writing under oath. If one party chooses to use interrogatories, the questions are sent to the lawyer representing the other side, and that party has a period of time in which to answer. Most states allow thirty days to answer interrogatories. Usually interrogatories are used for background information, because the respondent has thirty days to think before providing answers. This eliminates the element of surprise that exists in a deposition, in which a witness has to answer questions contemporaneously.

In addition to depositions and interrogatories, there are other discovery methods for obtaining evidence, such as requests for production of documents and requests for admissions by the opposing party. There are other methods for gathering evidence, but these are the four most common ways to obtain evidence before trial.

I knew from the very start that DuPont and Pine Island Farms weren't going to make things easy for us. In this case, the discovery process would be a long and tedious road designed to break us before we even saw the inside of a courtroom. The harder they made it for us to get evidence and the more they prolonged the process, the more time and money it would cost. The hope was that I'd break, give up, and walk away.

Fat chance.

I was in this to win this.

The two defendants made a tactical decision to split up their responsibilities when it came to providing certain types of evidence. The chemical titan DuPont took responsibility for all the science in the case, while Pine Island Farms took responsibility for defending against the alleged exposure to the DuPont product. Fortunately, this created a very defined separation between the science and the exposure to the product. The subsequent failure of the two defendants to allow for any overlap between the science and exposure would eventually play right into our hands.

Before we could get into any real discovery, we had one monumental, overriding task that required intervention by the judge. The problem we faced was an entirely unreasonable pretrial witness list served to us by DuPont and Pine Island. DuPont hit me with an initial list of over three hundred possible witnesses, hoping that the number and sheer workload involved would scare the crap out of me.

The case was brought before Judge Amy Steele Donner, a well-respected and highly seasoned judge who I thought would be very fair, given the many years of experience she'd had on the bench. She was known to be a no-nonsense judge, which was exactly what a case like this required.

By listing so many witnesses and knowing that we had the right, need, and necessity to depose each and every one them, our opponents were attempting to kill the case up front by making it impossible to pursue because it would require taking depositions every single day of the week except Sunday for over a year. But if they were going to play hardball, so was I.

Our first attempt to schedule depositions of the first few witnesses on the list was met with a total lack of cooperation and obstruction from both defendants. This led us to create a paper trail of communications with counsel documenting our attempts and their obstruction. This, in turn, led to us filing a motion before Judge Donner requesting judicial assistance in scheduling over three hundred witnesses for deposition.

At the hearing before Judge Donner, I showed up with a proposed schedule of depositions that laid out a five- or six-day-a-week plan spanning four countries over the course of the next year. The judge could tell the list was a tactic to bury us in discovery and forced the defendants' hand. She put their feet to the fire and demanded that they provide the addresses, especially for those who didn't have one listed for every single witness on their list, and she also gave us permission to set up the schedule over the course of the next year. And she made that final list of witnesses, including proper names and addresses, due within one week. She also warned both sides that if we couldn't agree on when things were going to happen, she was going to set strict deadlines. She made it clear that she wanted all the pretrial work completed within the next year or two at the latest. I told the judge I was ready to start and was willing to work every day, even if it meant going out of business. I stood straight-facedly in front of her and called DuPont's bluff every bit as much as she did.

A week later, they came back with a witness list that had been pared down to eighty-five people. After we had gone through the list with Judge Donner, we'd gotten it down to a total of sixty-three people, still located in four different countries. Little did I know at the time that my DuPont litigation (inclusive of the Castillo case and those of the twenty-nine Scottish families) would require forty trips to London over the next decade.

All in all, I'd say we won that battle.

Now the real work began.

The first thing we did was nail down the November 1989 exposure incident as described by Donna Castillo. It was clear from the outset that the farm was going to be incredibly uncooperative and obstructive at every turn. Tactically, I decided it would be best to take the deposition of Lynn Chaffin, the manager of the farm, without the benefit of any background interrogatories. Chaffin was a former high-end stockbroker who was hired in 1982 by Jack Wishart, the farm owner, because of his business knowledge and expertise. He became responsible for running the day-to-day operations at the fields, including the spraying program.

From looking at John Ashton's investigative reports for the *Observer*, I already knew there was a connection between the use of Benlate and ocular malformations. Ashton had called many farmers, including Chaffin, to see what mothers had been exposed to Benlate.

Ashton gave me a copy of his notes before I met with Chaffin, who wasn't your average farmer. He was a savvy businessman, who claimed he ran Pine Island Farms as a "hobby." We'd soon learn, Chaffin took his hobby very seriously. This wasn't someone who was in farming for fun; it was a serious business—and, as it turned out, a family business, because Chaffin is Wishart's son-in-law.

According to Ashton's notes, the call between Chaffin and the reporter took place on a specific day at 4:40 p.m. in the UK, where Ashton was calling from, which is 11:40 a.m. EST. The notes showed that the call lasted nine minutes. Chaffin's cellular phone number was clearly written on the single page of notes taken by Ashton, along with the words "used benomyl around November 1 or 2, 1989."

I suspected Chaffin might lie during the deposition, so I did what I could to pin him down on his answers. I started with a general conversation about his telephone numbers. I had his business, home, and cellular numbers and asked him about each one individually.

"Is this your home number?"

"Yes."

"Who uses your home phone?"

"My wife, kids, or anyone else who is around the house."

"Is this your business number?"

"Yup."

"Who uses your business phone?"

"Sometimes my secretary, workers at the farm . . ."

"What about your cell phone? Is this your number?"

Chaffin paused. "Yes."

"And can you tell me, Mr. Chaffin, who uses that number?"

"Just me."

"No one else uses it?"

"No, just me."

I got him to admit he was the *only* user of the number Ashton called. I didn't try to get this background information with interrogatories, because he would have had thirty days to think about his answers and their possible ramifications. Hitting him with it this way was far more productive.

I circled back to the day of the Ashton call.

"Do you recall getting a call from a reporter named John Ashton on this particular day? He had a heavy English accent and the call lasted nearly ten minutes," I said.

"No, no recollection of that at all."

Chaffin's cell phone records clearly supported Ashton's claim that he called at 11:40 a.m. EST and spoke with Chaffin for nine minutes. Unfortunately, Chaffin's cell phone records only showed an incoming call without disclosing the number of the incoming caller—Ashton.

Hoping he'd admit that the call took place, I put the cell phone document in front of him and asked, "Does this refresh your memory? It shows a nine-minute incoming call at the exact time Ashton states he spoke to you. Are you sure you don't remember that call?"

"Nope. No recollection."

There's no doubt Chaffin understood that the document showed only an incoming call to his number. Since it didn't state who it was from, he gambled—big-time—by continuing to deny the call with Ashton ever took place. This meant I would have to get Ashton's phone records to prove it.

Asking for phone records from the *Observer* would prove to be harder than I expected, because they're an overseas newspaper. It would require a year of subpoenas and going through the Hague Convention to get prior approval. It wasn't easy. It took time and effort, but I eventually obtained the records. A year later, with Ashton's phone records in hand, I scheduled a continuation of Chaffin's deposition. This time I could prove the identity of the incoming caller to Chaffin's cell phone number. Chaffin was clearly unaware that I had obtained this critical information.

"A year ago I asked you about an English reporter. I know you're worked up over this case—thinking about it all the time . . ."

"Yeah."

"So I want to ask you again: do you remember taking this call?"

"No."

"Let me refresh your memory."

I then gave Chaffin the same cell phone records I had given him the year before. This time, however, I also provided him with a copy of the detailed bill listing all the calls made from Ashton's phone line at the *Observer*, provided to me by Centel, the *Observer*'s telephone company.

Obviously, Chaffin would now be forced to admit that the call took place.

"The records show the call the reporter has spoken about was made to your cell phone. Want to take a look?"

"Maybe I thought it was a sales call. Maybe I was misleading the guy," Chaffin said.

Despite being cornered, Chaffin still didn't want to give up.

"Let me get this straight, Mr. Chaffin. You thought it was a sales call and you stayed on the phone for nine minutes? Most people duck sales calls by hanging up. But you, you stayed on the phone to deliberately mislead and lie to this guy?"

Greg Gaebe, Chaffin's lawyer who was present for the deposition, jumped in and exclaimed, "He never said 'lied.'"

That was true, but then I asked Chaffin, "What is the difference between lying and misleading to you, Mr. Chaffin?"

"There is no difference."

Basically, Chaffin was busted. The call clearly took place, and now everyone knew it.

At this point I thought any jury would see Chaffin for what he was: a liar. Furthermore, any jury would believe Benlate was used on the farm on November 1 or 2, 1989.

Despite the milestone success in busting Chaffin, there was still a huge problem: Benlate is an odorless, tasteless, and colorless spray. We still needed to prove that the liquid that came out of the big sprayer attachment with the thirty-six-foot wingspan described by Donna Castillo in my office and in her depositions was, in fact, Benlate.

Strategically, I needed to show that the farm not only had Benlate at the time but also that they actually used it in the manner Donna had described. It was important to know what chemicals the farm had on hand and was using then. This meant that we had to get their purchase records through a request for production. I was able to narrow my search to two suppliers that sold the farm its chemicals during that period of time. Unfortunately, one of them had lost all their records during Hurricane Andrew, the strongest hurricane to ever hit south Florida. Andrew wiped out communities south of Miami, killing fifteen people when it struck in 1992. Dozens more died from injuries stemming from the storm and its aftermath.

The other supplier had provided Benlate to the farm in May 1989. It was reasonable to believe that the farm still had a supply of it in November. Unfortunately, their records showed that the farm also had a total of sixty-four other chemicals on hand then, too, including herbicides, insecticides, fungicides, nutrients, and water. The task at hand now was to determine how many of the sixty-five chemicals, if any, were odorless, tasteless, and colorless and would have been applied with the thirty-six-foot sprayer attachment.

We had already ruled out water because when I deposed Chaffin, I asked him how they watered the crops. He explained that it was done with a water cannon, which shoots water at the crops. It doesn't come from a tractor with a sprayer attachment. So with that admission, we immediately knew whatever Donna had been soaked in wasn't water.

We had also ruled out nutrients, because I had asked Chaffin about how the farm provided nutrients to its crops. He explained that the nutrients were put into a planned water irrigation system, then applied directly to the root zone of the plants by means of applicators (orifices, emitters, porous tubing, perforated pipes, etc.) placed either on or below the surface of the ground and operated under low pressure.

Furthermore, we were able to eliminate all herbicides from our list of possibilities, because based on Chaffin's deposition, the farm used a special tractor with a twelve-foot wingspan for spraying them.

That left us with about twenty insecticides and fungicides to focus on. Most of those had an odor or some kind of taste, but there were five that were odorless, tasteless, and colorless and appeared to be just like water.

The good news was that we had narrowed the list of sixty-five chemicals to only five possible culprits.

The bad news was that we had to prove Benlate, as opposed to the other agents, was *the* cause.

We were about a year away from our scheduled trial date, and I still needed to figure out how I was going to solve this problem. While I had eliminated the bulk of the possibilities, there were still five potential fungicides or insecticides the farmer could have been using the day Donna was sprayed.

If the farm simply said they were using all five, we were fucked. Game over. Case closed.

There would be no way for us to say which one of the five she had been hit with, because the burden of proof was on us. It was incumbent on me to prove by the greater weight of the evidence that it was Benlate. What I mean by *proving the greater weight of the evidence* is that it has to be a greater-than-fifty-percent chance it was Benlate, or we could never get in front of the jury. A one-in-five shot is only 20 percent, and not enough to win the case.

It felt as though the whole case was about to go down the tubes.

By the time I got to this point, I was already two years into discovery and had a boatload of time and money sunk into this case. I spent endless days and nights wracking my brain, trying to figure out how I was going to prove it was Benlate that had been coming from the damn tractor with the thirty-six-foot sprayer attachment. There was no chance Chaffin would knowingly admit it or that the worker driving the tractor would remember. Too much time had passed, and too much was at stake.

It occurred to me about a year before trial that the only solid chance we had left to save the case was to use requests for admissions. These are simply statements of fact that either side prepares and that the opposing party must admit or deny. You design your own requests for admissions, and the opposing party has thirty days to reply. The answers provided by them become absolute irrefutable facts that can be used against them at trial. The only problem is that, just like interrogatories, the answering party has thirty days to reflect and think about their response. For this reason, I had to be very tactical about when I would send the requests. I needed to catch the other side off guard.

It was during a particularly tumultuous deposition, where both DuPont's and Pine Island's attorneys were being so obstructive and obstinate that they were instructing their clients not to answer many of my questions (refusing even to provide us with their business address!), that the lights went on in my head. This was the perfect time to prepare and serve requests for admissions. It was a year before trial, and both defendants were clearly in total denial mode about every facet of the case. They were putting up brick walls at every turn, thinking that would cause me to cave. With so much time left before the trial, neither defendant appeared especially focused on the big picture—certainly not like I was, or as they should have been at the time.

Our only hope was that they would take their current denial mentality to the next level. Maybe they would neglect to think things through properly and simply deny my requests for admissions. If they were dumb enough to do that, they'd be stuck holding the position that none of the other products came out of the tractor with the thirty-six-foot sprayer attachment on the day in question. That position would be binding.

In other words, the one who makes an admission cannot suddenly change their mind or say, "That's not what I meant." It is what it is, and it's done. It becomes an absolute fact.

It was a risk, but it was definitely worth a shot. "What the hell?" I thought.

So I wrote up sixty-five requests for admissions, each one a single line asking the defendants to "admit or deny they were using **Benlate** on or about November 1 or 2, 1989"; "admit or deny they were using **Trigard** on or about November 1 or 2, 1989"; "admit or deny they were using **Bravo** on or about November 1 or 2, 1989"; and so on until I had individually listed all sixty-five chemicals the farm had had on hand.

I put the requests for admissions in a package, crossed my fingers, and mailed it out.

Waiting those thirty days for their responses was like waiting for a jury verdict. I was on pins and needles, hoping and praying for denials across the board. If they all came back as admissions, we were screwed. While you can use the answers that are favorable to you against the opponent, you can also throw the ones that don't work for you in the garbage. But even if the responses were not helpful and I threw them all away, I didn't know how else I could prove it was Benlate and not any of those other sixty-four agents. To pull this off, our only hope was to get denials across the board.

Thirty long and painful days of waiting later, we received their answers.

They denied everything.

*Everything!*

I turned to my team and said, "Holy shit. Look at this. This is fucking awesome. They did it. They fell right into our trap!"

This was a huge break for us. As far as litigation went, this was a great—albeit lucky—move.

I mean *very* lucky.

It was also a game changer. It was one of those moments when I had to take a shot—be all in or get the hell out.

Thankfully, it worked. They had no idea what they'd done, and I had no intention of tipping them off until we got to trial.

# 7

DuPont had known for a long time that Benlate was dangerous. There had been ongoing litigation over the same product for several years before we filed the Castillo case, because the harmful chemical was destroying farmers' harvests. Interestingly, the way Benlate extinguished crops mirrored the way it damaged human eyes. As a species, we have something in our cells called tubulin, which is also present in plants. Benlate is a spindle poison that inhibits the growth of tubulin. It finds the tubulin in the cells of fungus and kills it. Unfortunately for DuPont, it works on both humans and plants in the same way. That is exactly what showed up in the 1991 University of California study, too.

What I wanted to find out next was whether DuPont had done studies of their own that showed similar harmful results. After all, they created the poisonous product. They must have done some research or had some documentation that showed results similar to those of the University of California studies.

I knew DuPont had a document depository in Delaware, where their corporate offices were located, which they had created during the crop litigation. They kept millions of documents filed there in a large warehouse building where lawyers could look for whatever they thought they needed for their cases. The depository was intimidating, imposing, huge, poorly organized (at least for us!), and very dusty. The first time I walked in I just wanted to turn around and go home. My only thought was that I could spend ten years there and still barely make a dent.

To make matters worse, this was before the digital age, so all the files were paper files, which meant we had to physically wade through each and every potential page of evidence by hand. There were hundreds of thousands of pages, if not more, that we had to get through. The depository had a librarian on staff whose sole job was to make opposing lawyers' lives miserable. She fit the classic librarian stereotype: gray hair, a bit frumpy. While she appeared to be kind and accommodating, her real mission was to confuse, mislead, and disarm the opponent. To her, anyone outside the DuPont family was the enemy.

While there was an index of documents, it was extremely difficult to understand, unless of course you were the one who compiled it. It made little sense to anyone other than the librarian and a handful of DuPont insiders. That was the point.

My team consisted of Marjorie Salem and myself. Marjorie, an associate who worked for me, spent endless hours delving into old boxes that had been hidden away for years. We could have sat there endlessly, with no promise of ever coming up with what we were look-ing for. Nothing was properly labeled or logically filed. There was no rhyme or reason to what was handed over to us, which I suspected was very much by design.

This is what is known as a classic document dump. Defendants are required to cooperate by giving you access to their documents, but they aren't required to make it easy. "Here you go. You figure it out."

Yeah, right.

Whenever we asked for a specific document, the librarian's answer was always, "No, we don't have that study," or "If we do have that study, it might be in this area over here," or "Did you look over there?" and she'd wave her hand in the general direction of more boxes taking up space in the large, dark, and dreary warehouse building. Sure, she provided some assistance, but nothing was ever where it was supposed to be.

Finally, we realized that if she sent us to the right, we ought to check out whatever was to the left. If she said look up, we should look down. We'd go to wherever she told us to search and begin by looking around the edges, then work our way out and back in again. Odds were that whatever we were looking for—especially if it was the rat studies on Benlate or benomyl—we were not going to find it there. And if the studies *were* there, they weren't going to be clearly labeled "Rat Studies."

We did, however, find some in vitro tests and dermal skin transmission studies that proved to be important elements in our case. The in vitro tests showed the level of exposure to benomyl at which cells die, and the dermal skin transmission studies showed what percentage of the chemical could permeate human skin. The in vitro test results were good for us, because they illustrated that at the very low dose of twenty-two parts per billion of benomyl, cells die. This is what causes malformations. And the dermal skin transmissions studies illustrated that 3 percent of the amount of the chemical that gets on a person's skin makes its way into their bloodstream. This was solid information and would help our case, but what we really needed to find were those rat studies.

As mentioned earlier, the biggest obstacle was the filing index. Documents were not filed in any rational manner. To the contrary— they were intentionally filed in an irrational manner so that critical documents would be nearly impossible to find. It became clear to us that while critical documents were filed in a way that kept them hidden from outsiders, there still had to be a system in place to make sure they were properly mislaid. Otherwise, how would the librarian know how to misdirect us?

Shortly before we were about to pack it in, I stumbled across a stack of papers marked "Special Luncheon Memo(s)" that had several attachments stapled to them. These appeared to be suspiciously out of place, so I began flipping through them, one page after the other.

BINGO!

"Hey, look at this!" I shouted across the room to Marjorie. "I think I found the rat studies!"

And I had.

They were the studies Robert Staples, the head of toxicology for DuPont, had conducted in 1980 and 1982, cleverly hidden under special luncheon memos where no one else was likely to search. Clearly, we needed to take Staples's deposition. I now felt that we were in a strong enough position to make our case—that it was a good a time to pull the trigger and let the show begin.

After three weeks of combing through hundreds of thousands of pages, I came up with eighty thousand pages of relevant material that I wanted to use, and I earmarked it as evidence. When I told the librarian about my needs, she smiled and said, "No problem." I figured they'd send me a bill for the usual ten cents a page, along with copies of everything I had put aside.

Marjorie and I left Delaware and waited for the eighty thousand pages we had selected to arrive. We needed those documents, which DuPont had to deliver to us within a certain window of time to be compliant. They agreed to send the documents; however, they sent me a bill for $80,000, which was equivalent to a dollar a page, not the standard ten cents a page I was used to paying everywhere else. When the bill arrived, I thought it had to be some kind of mistake. Surely they had made an error. But they hadn't. The cover letter stated that I was required to pay the full amount in advance or they wouldn't send me the documents. DuPont knew we were under a tight discovery schedule, with several pending motions that could kill our case without those documents.

I went bat-shit crazy and began bitching and complaining to my staff like a lunatic on the loose, which is exactly what they expected me to do. Regardless, I didn't want DuPont to perceive any weakness on our side. I contemplated going to the judge, but we didn't have the time—nor was there any assurance it would help. After some deep thought and deliberation, I decided I would turn their hoped-for weakness into a strength.

Even though it would put a financial strain on me and I wasn't happy about it, I prepared a check for the full amount and placed it in a FedEx envelope to go out that day. I put a one-line note inside that read, "Enclosed you will find a check in the amount of $80,000—I expect the documents as agreed by 5:00 p.m. tomorrow."

This was part of the DuPont litigation strategy. Make the case impossible at every turn, both physically and financially. I'd heard from a friend that they had been snooping around, looking up my tax returns to see just how far they could financially push me and our firm. Thankfully, we were still making really good money. Little did they know that I could and would endure their wrath, come hell or high water. It had been made very clear who I was dealing with—a bunch of ruthless bastards who were out to ruin me before I could take them down for what they had done to little Johnny Castillo. From where I stood, that just meant they were worried because they knew I was on to them and had a good shot at winning this case. It was only after I paid for the documents that I think the defense lawyers began treating me with a little respect. None of their nonsense was working, and they must have realized that I was crazy enough to see this through to the bitter end.

While the results of the Staples studies weren't quite as bad as those of the University of California study, they certainly weren't good. It appeared that Staples had tested the product in two different studies and got two different results.

DuPont had been trying to get their product licensed since 1977. At the time they conducted the 1980 study they had a Rebuttable

Presumption Against Registration (RPAR) that they needed to warn pregnant women about possible birth defects caused by exposure to Benlate. To lift the RPAR, DuPont needed to prove that their product was safe. The 1980 Staples study did not accomplish that. So DuPont went back and repeated the study in 1982, but this time the results were much better. Purportedly it was the same study, but all of a sudden the results were much better, because they weren't finding as many malformations this time around.

We were baffled by the differing results.

Armed with the 80,000 pages of documentation from DuPont, I was able to take Staples's deposition. In preparing for that deposition, I smelled a rat—and it wasn't a lab rat. There had to be something different in those studies. I wracked my brain, reading and rereading the studies and the underlying data until it finally came to me. One study was histological, and the other was clinical. A histological study is better, because it's carried out with a microscope, and the measurement (in this case, of the eyes) is actually calculated mathematically. If the eyes were undersized, they were called microphthalmic, which means there was a negative effect—the eyes didn't grow enough and it was considered a malformation.

In contrast, clinical studies are based largely on opinion: some guy in a lab is saying, "Looks good to me." He is essentially eyeballing the results and then moving on to the next rat. You can easily get better results from a test like that than you can when you are conducting a mathematically based histological study.

Finally, when scientists conduct these studies, they compare milligrams of the chemical to kilograms of body weight (mg/kg). In a well-designed study, the rats will be weighed every day. Rats aren't like humans; they grow really fast, which means their weight can change very quickly. This can radically affect the ratio of milligrams to kilograms. In the more scientific 1980 Staples study, the rats were weighed daily, which provided a true and accurate comparison of dose to weight measurement. In 1982, however, they were *not* weighed daily, and therefore the information in this second study produced artificially better results for DuPont and could not be considered anywhere near as accurate as the 1980 study. Staples admitted the methodology was good for the 1980 study but couldn't explain why the results were so bad. His only attempted explanation for the improved results in 1982 was the availability of better "computer technology." However, when we eventually pressed Staples in his deposition, he admitted that the two studies had different methodologies and that the preliminary report he prepared in 1980 wasn't so good for DuPont. The results showed signs of eye malformations at very low testing levels. As it turned out, Staples caught a lot of heat from his superiors—even though he was the head of toxicology—for preparing the report without prior review from the higher-ups in the company.

Marjorie and I felt we had struck gold when we found those rat studies—especially the Staples studies. Now, after the depositions, it was clear that in fact we had.

"You're the best, Jim," she said.

I heard this from her often, which felt good.

Really good.

# 8

MARJORIE WAS A young, up-and-coming lawyer who had worked for me for six years. She was smart and beautiful and thought the sun rose and set on me. She was six years younger than me and extremely fit, and we shared a lot in common. She was eager to please—in every way. I didn't mind, even though I knew I was breaking my marriage vows. I'd been putting in so much time at the office for years that I rarely spent any time at home with my wife or my kids. Something was definitely changing at home, and in my relationship with Diane. For me, things began to change when my firm was struggling back in 1987 and I wasn't getting the support at home that I wanted from my wife. At the time, she was encouraging me to shut down my practice and join a large, established law firm. I wanted her to believe in me as much as I did; when she didn't, I felt like an outsider in our relationship. I know it couldn't have been easy for her to be on her own while I worked eighteen hours or more a day. Working weekends was common, too. What woman wants that kind of relationship? I felt bad, I really did. Yet Marjorie had ways of making me feel good. She was constantly telling me how smart I was, what a good lawyer I was, and how attractive she found me. She became irresistible.

In the three years we'd worked on discovery for the Castillo case, Marjorie and I had spent a lot of time together and had grown quite close. She went to most of the depositions with me, and while I was the one who deposed the witness, I liked having her there by my side. I never told her I would leave my wife, nor did I promise that our relationship was more than it was. I was careful to be clear about how I felt. I loved my wife and children.

Regardless of our personal relationship, Marjorie never wavered from her professional obligations during this time. She was a tremendous help, and knew the case almost as well as I did. We were a team. I was going to have her at the trial, as she would easily be able to handle some of the workload and give me a breather here and there. I thought it would help me survive the onslaught from DuPont's dozen lawyers. Knowing she was in my corner and ready to assist was a huge relief to me.

As my career took off and our family dynamic changed, Diane's and my relationship had slowly drifted away from what it once was. Although we weren't the kind of couple who got into crazy screaming matches or who constantly argued, we had, sadly, become the kind of couple who preferred staying independently busy and spending an increasing amount of time apart.

I knew Diane and I were in trouble when I agreed to take the Castillo case. I don't think it was a factor in my saying yes. In fact, I'm certain I said yes because every time I looked at my children I was reminded that I felt called to serve a higher purpose in my life. I believed lawyers are supposed to take what they do seriously and work to make a positive difference in people's lives. While we don't take a Hippocratic Oath like doctors do, I always felt it was my job and my responsibility to seek justice for those who couldn't do it themselves. I suppose this altruistic approach to my profession comes with a high price, especially when working on the time-consuming types of cases I do.

In the fall of 1995, the ultimate cost was the demise of my marriage. After eighteen years together, Diane and I realized we were no longer compatible as husband and wife. We were two different people, and as a result we separated on October 1 of that year. I moved to a small furnished condo in Coconut Grove. It came decorated with cheap bamboo furniture, a far cry from the comfortable and well-appointed home Diane and I had created together for our family. I was living a spartan existence by choice. I think I was subconsciously punishing myself for my pending divorce.

Leaving my children and moving out of our family home was by far the hardest decision I had ever made. It left me with an empty feeling deep inside my soul. My father had instilled in me from a very early age a meaningful sense of family. I didn't want to disappoint anyone, especially Diane or the kids.

Before I moved out, I came clean with Diane about my affair with Marjorie. I didn't like lying to her or hiding behind closed doors. It wasn't fair to anyone. While I never promised Marjorie a future, I had taken vows with Diane. I felt confessing was the right thing to do. As difficult and painful as the truth was to tell, I wanted Diane to know everything. She didn't deserve to be hurt more than I had already hurt her.

Once Diane and I separated, I also wanted Marjorie to understand that while I may have left Diane, it didn't mean I was moving closer to her. In fact, it was quite the opposite. After I made the decision to leave my wife, I wanted more freedom to see other people. Marjorie didn't take this revelation well, but I didn't care. Throughout our relationship I had been clear that I never planned to divorce my wife. And that was the God's honest truth at the time. Even when we separated, I wasn't sure Diane and I would actually divorce. Besides, my focus couldn't be on marital issues; it had to be on the trial, which was just six months away. My only sanity came from my morning run. I woke up early each morning and ran six miles from Coconut Grove over the bridge on the Rickenbacker Causeway and back. I would get lost in my thoughts about the trial, the evidence, and anything else that was pertinent during those runs. Outside of work, it was the only outlet I allowed myself, and man, did I need it. I breathed in the fresh air, filling my lungs and feeding my body with oxygen so my mind would be sharp and I could stay physically strong. I felt like a warrior in training for the fight of my life. As the clock ticked, the pressure was definitely building, and I could feel it with every heartbeat before, during, and after my run.

While we were preparing for trial, I continued working on other cases and representing some professional football players, too. For the most part, though, my primary focus during the fall of 1995 was on being a trial lawyer. I was making a lot more money and getting much more satisfaction representing people who were really sick than from representing football players. Only a handful of pro-athlete clients were left at the firm by then, only because they were good enough players to make it worth our time. By the end of 1995, I had grown tired of dealing with the kind of athletes who were reckless in the off-season or careless with their finances. I was fed up with taking frivolous calls 24/7 or bailing guys out at three in the morning. It also seemed useless to negotiate on behalf of guys on NFL teams operating under salary caps. In other words, we were trying to get more money for our guy than the next guy, even though the teams were spending the same amount on all their players combined.

Gene Mato was a kid who came to work for me as a recruiter in the sports management company I had set up, and was someone I considered a bit of a loose cannon. On November 30, 1995, he called to tell me he was out with Danyell Ferguson, a superstar running back at the University of Miami who had already announced that he was going pro a year early. Mato said they were at Hooters in Coconut Grove and asked me if I would like to stop by and meet him. Danyell was a junior at Miami and looked like he had a very promising career ahead of him, so I agreed to stop by for a quick handshake and hello. In sports management, it's all about the relationships you create for the future.

When I arrived, I could see Mato and Ferguson had been drinking quite a bit. I made a little small talk, ate a chicken sandwich, and downed a beer before taking Mato aside and saying, "Listen. This kid is wasted. Make sure you get him home safe. Don't fuck this up, got it?"

I said good-bye to the boys and headed on my way.

Gene called the limo company our law firm used and gave them the corporate account number for billing. The driver showed up and drove them home. On the way, the guys asked if they could book a car for the next night, too.

"Sure," the driver said.

The driver showed up the next night as requested and picked up Danyell and two of his football buddies, receivers Jammi German and Yatil Green. At the end of the night, the driver asked to be paid. It was four in the morning, and the guys were drunk. They assured the driver they would "take care of him," but then suddenly opened the car door and ran away.

Instead of calling the dispatcher to report what happened, the driver called the police. If he had called the dispatcher, his boss would have told him not to worry about it. My firm had a big account with the limo company, and the driver would have been paid. But because the police were involved, it eventually became front-page news. Months later, an investigative reporter for the *Miami Herald* saw the police report involving University of Miami football players, my law firm, and our sports management company and thought, "This will make an interesting story."

Well after the incident had occurred, I picked up the Sunday paper, still groggy, and opened it as I usually did.

WILD LIMO RIDE WITH SPORTS AGENT

Yep.

That was the headline that greeted me as I sat innocently sipping my coffee. Worse, the type was the same size and font as the headline had been the day Princess Diana died.

It didn't register at first that this sensational headline could possibly have anything to do with me. Surely this was going to be some tragic and horrific story about a wild night that didn't end well for the parties involved.

As I began to read the story, I could feel the blood rush through my body. And it was *boiling*.

I didn't know if I was pissed or embarrassed or both.

I was newly single and didn't want Diane to think I had anything to do with this mess or for her to misconstrue the situation. All I could think was, "So what? A couple of kids ran out on their limo bill? How is this news?" Naturally, I wouldn't run out on a limo bill, but these were a couple of college kids out carousing and having a good time.

Was it right?

Hell no.

But did the *Miami Herald* have to make such a salacious story of it? According to their report, during that second night, the limo driver ended up as a backseat passenger. One of the players wore the driver's cap and drove the car around while the other players were drinking and having sex with their girlfriends in the back. But here's what really got me fired up: even though I was not there when it happened and didn't know about it at the time, the *Herald* story made it sound as though I was smack in the middle of it all.

From a legal point of view, I couldn't understand why this had become front-page news. The night in question had come shortly after the NCAA's Infractions Committee banned the University of Miami from playing in a bowl game that season for eight categories of rules violations, but none of that had anything to do with the incident or our firm. In fact, since Miami wasn't playing in a bowl game, it allowed us to talk to those players who had exhausted their eligibility to play college football. Ferguson had already announced he was forgoing his senior year to turn pro, so that made him fair game.

However, the limo incident blew up to be such a big thing because a new Florida statute, enacted only sixty days prior to the night in question, made it a third-degree felony to operate as a sports agent without a Florida state license. While I had the state license, the statute also stated that it was a third-degree felony to "aid or abet an unlicensed agent by recruiting or soliciting" college football players. Whether Gene was licensed was irrelevant, because he was "recruiting and soliciting" these guys for me, a licensed agent, and he was operating in full compliance with the law. But that's not how the state saw it.

Some young prosecutor decided to come after me because my *company* (as opposed to me) was not licensed, despite the fact that under the statute you can't license a company—you can only license individuals.

This story hit the papers, and now, just months before the Castillo case was set to go to trial, I was facing criminal and NCAA investigations as well as a media frenzy.

I've often wondered if this case would have been brought against me if I hadn't taken the Castillo case. Sometimes in life we bring these things on ourselves whether we mean to or not. High-profile lawyers can easily become targets both in the media and in their communities. People love to see the big guy fall, no matter if it's the president, a beloved movie star, or a favorite pro athlete.

I hired my friend and colleague Roy Black to represent me against the allegations my firm and I were being charged with in the criminal case. I absolutely denied having anything to do with ordering the limo or recruiting these students. Of course, the implications of these allegations were far-reaching, because the three students involved could become ineligible to play ball going forward. I didn't want to be responsible for the long-lasting impact on these boy's lives a night of frivolous joyriding ending in an unpaid $1,032.00 limo bill could have had. There was no wrongdoing on anyone's part, and I certainly wasn't willing to see these three talented guys' lives destroyed by the NCAA or by an overaggressive prosecutor who was trying to take me down over something that was really nothing. The guys came up with the money to make restitution within a couple of days of this thing making the news and admitted they had made some bad decisions that night. Under different circumstances, this would all have been smoothed over without a media circus. But that wasn't the case this time.

I found myself dealing with "Limogate," my separation, and preparations for the biggest trial of my life all at the same time. For reasons I'll never understand, Mato ran scared and made a misdemeanor deal with the state, agreeing to be wired in an attempt to entrap me and gain information that could be used against me. Fortunately, there was nothing I could say that would be helpful to the state, because nothing criminal happened. Even so, I found it amusing that Mato tried to take me down. He would come into my office from time to time asking if we could talk about the limo case. Each time I answered him the same way, saying, "There's nothing to talk about. You were a moron for putting those boys into a limousine without getting in yourself to make sure they got home safely."

Calling my stress levels high would be a gross understatement. And still, none of it really jarred me. I was in warrior mode all the way.

It took two years and hundreds of thousands of dollars in legal fees to prove our innocence and retain our right to continue working in sports management, but we were eventually victorious. When all was said and done, it was my personal Oliver North moment that truly redeemed me in this mess. The Florida Bar is always the last step in the process after all criminal and civil agencies. The Bar held a probable cause hearing, which could have jeopardized my license to practice law if things didn't go well. Since there was a lot of media attention on this case, the Bar assigned a separate federal prosecutor to investigate for six months before the hearing. It turns out that early on, the NCAA, as part of their own investigation, came to my office to question me about the incident with the football players. When they asked me if I knew the players in question, I said I didn't. That was a lie. It wasn't a lie under oath, but it wasn't the truth. The reason I chose to lie was because, at the time, the NCAA was known to go on what I felt were crazy witch hunts that unfairly destroyed young football players' careers. In fact, the *Yale Law Journal* had published an extensive article that went into great length and detail about the NCAA, its haphazard fishing expeditions or investigations, and the negative effects they often had on innocent student athletes. I knew that if I had answered honestly, it may have jeopardized the guys' future prospects of playing professional football.

At the probable cause hearing, the federal prosecutor asked me if it was true that I had met with the NCAA in the summer of 1996.

"Yes." I said. I knew where he was going with his questions.

"Isn't it true that you told the NCAA that you had never met the players?"

"Yes."

"Wasn't that a lie?" he asked, thinking I would stick with my story.

"Yes," I said, bewildering the prosecutor.

"Why did you lie to the NCAA?" he asked, flustered by my honesty.

I went on to explain my reasoning to him and the panel in excruciating detail, including my feelings about the *Yale Law Journal* article and the NCAA. While I didn't go so far as to state that "I did it for my country," I did let them know I wasn't about to allow innocent players to become victims of yet another of the NCAA's witch hunts, which were common at the time.

Immediately after the testimony, my lawyer who I had retained to handle the Florida Bar case, Jack Weiss, and I were asked to wait outside while they deliberated. We were just on the other side of the door, so I could overhear everything. One member of the panel said, "I think what he did was honorable."

Another member said, "But he lied."

And yet another panel member said, "But what he did was honorable."

With that, Jack said, "Let's get away from the door."

He was right. We didn't need to stand there and listen to what was going down.

Ten minutes later, the panel came back with a finding of no probable cause, which put a victorious end to this whole ridiculous saga.

# 9

As the Castillo trial drew closer, I became a man possessed. There was still so much work to do before going to court. I had expert witnesses I needed to depose, and I felt there weren't enough hours in my day to get it all done before the start date in April.

In a way, I was grateful for the distraction of the case. It became oddly cathartic for me with Limogate and my separation, which by now had become my impending divorce. My failed marriage caused a lot of emotional grief for me. Having such a heavy workload provided something to focus on. If I immersed myself in the tasks at hand, I didn't have to think about anything else.

After finding the rat studies, Marjorie and I knew we had to track down Robert Staples to take his deposition. It took some time, but our private investigator ultimately located him. He was living in Delaware and was now retired. As the author of the two studies, he had the potential to become a key witness for us. After all, he was the head of toxicology for DuPont during the period that these studies took place.

He wrote the preliminary report in 1980 stating that the results were not good, which meant DuPont knew their product had issues.

Staples turned out to be a very approachable and kind man, although he wasn't totally forthcoming about why the results in his studies were bad. He never gave me a really good explanation, other than to say, "We ran the study in 1982 and the results were better because the computer technology was better."

Given the differences in the studies, he knew it was a bullshit answer, and so did I.

During his deposition, however, Staples told me that when he met with the higher-ups at DuPont after his damning preliminary report on the 1980 study, they said to him, "Listen, we don't want you to be a Lone Ranger. We want our input in the final report, not yours."

When I asked why they were calling him a "lone ranger," he explained that it was because he wrote the initial report without them.

I was baffled by his response, because as the head of toxicology, wasn't it his job to report his findings? When I asked him this question, he said it was his job, and he found it odd that they would ask him to do anything other than speak the truth.

"The Lone Ranger always speaks the truth, right?" he said.

I had to agree.

While I was satisfied with what I got from his testimony, I wasn't convinced Staples would make a great witness on the stand. He wasn't overwhelmingly convincing one way or the other, even if his studies leaned in our direction. Also, I didn't feel his personality was engaging enough for him to be an ally of ours. For whatever reason, he still appeared to have an allegiance to DuPont—or, at the very least, to the studies conducted during his tenure there. By the time I finished with his deposition, I felt I had enough evidence through his testimony, which I would read to the jury without ever putting Staples on the stand. Staples clearly helped our cause.

Every time we presented evidence to the judge that could be used as scientific backup, DuPont referred to it as "junk science." They called *everything* junk science, and even tried to force us into finding and producing studies that didn't or couldn't realistically exist. For example, they wanted us to come up with a controlled epidemiological study, which would make perfect sense if we were testing a drug, because drugs, as explained before, can be tested on pregnant women, whereas chemicals can't. To produce an epidemiological study, I would have had to find pregnant women who were exposed to this chemical during the critical part of their pregnancies (the seven-to-ten-week period) to prove that the same result occurred for them as occurred for my client. A study like that would have cost tens of millions of dollars. How do you even perform that type of study? We would have had to find women who were unwillingly and randomly exposed, as Donna was. In fact, Donna *was* my study. And yet the lawyers for DuPont argued that since there were no good epidemiological studies, the evidence should not be allowed.

Well, they had a point.

There were no epidemiological studies.

The fact was, I didn't need an epidemiological study to prove the science. Instead, I assembled a stellar team of thirteen scientists to establish our case piece by piece, and I made sure the team included a fetal pathologist—someone who could speak to the jury about what happened to Johnny while he was in the womb.

Having a fetal pathologist testify was extremely important, because it would help the jury understand how the chemical generally got through the skin to the cells of the fetus. The easiest way to lose the case was to have one scientist act as a jack-of-all-trades. Each scientist had to cover a very defined aspect of the case based on both their specialized expertise and generally accepted science.

Finding a fetal pathologist who could speak to the issues was no easy task. We literally had to trace the path the chemical took from its point of contact with Donna's skin through her dermal layer, into her bloodstream, through the placenta, and right down to the embryo's cells.

I was on a business trip to London when Alan Care, a British solicitor who I knew and who I sometimes worked with on chemical cases in Great Britain, suggested I meet with a professor at the University of Liverpool by the name of Dr. Vyvyan Howard. I would later find out that Dr. Howard was a developmental toxicologist, also called a teratologist, which is someone who studies birth defects. His training was in fetal pathology, which made him an ideal witness for the case because of his specialty in breaking every detail down into molecules. He was obviously extremely smart, and appeared to be quite good natured despite being a bit socially awkward.

If you were to conjure up an image of the quintessential scientist, Dr. Howard would fit the description. He was a stout man with a big belly, frizzy red hair, and wire-rimmed glasses that fell to the tip of his nose. If he wasn't studying in a lab, I'd almost expect to find him drinking in an Irish pub and sounding off on the latest scientific theory. He just struck me as one of those guys. We became very good friends during the discovery phase of the case. Unfortunately, he had little to no experience in a courtroom. I spent days doing my best to prepare him, but despite all that preparation, I had a bit of a scare the night before one of his depositions. I made the mistake of sending my associate Ana Rivero to meet with Dr. Howard for a final review the day before one of his depositions. I flew to London that night to join Dr. Howard and Ana at the Ritz for dinner and one last conference. When I arrived, the first words out of Ana's mouth were, "We have a problem."

"What's the problem?" I asked.

"Dr. Howard can't testify to the exposure."

"What do you mean he can't testify to the exposure?"

"He can't give us a number; he can't do it." Ana was in an absolute panic.

"What do you mean he can't give us a number? He can't say it's, like, fifty-seven parts per billion or something, based on the exposure?"

"No, he can't say that for sure." She was terrified that we had no case without him.

After a very brief but powerful head rush, I asked Dr. Howard if he could forget about providing a specific number. We knew for a fact that when the exposure is twenty-two parts per billion, the cells die. We also knew that at three parts per billion, neurite retraction occurs, and cells lose their ability to communicate with one another. What we really needed Dr. Howard to do was show that, based on the exposure the plaintiff had to the chemical, the amount that reached the embryo was in excess of twenty-two parts per billion—or at least three parts per billion.

"If you can't give us a precise number, can you say that the exposure described by Donna was in the hundreds of parts per billion?" I asked.

"Oh, absolutely, absolutely. Oh, yeah. No, clearly it was in the hundreds of parts per billion." He said this with great conviction.

Perhaps we were getting somewhere.

"Could it have been in the thousands of parts per billion—which is parts per million?" I asked.

"Absolutely," he replied.

"So when I give you the hypothetical scenario, could your answer be that it's 'in the hundreds of parts per billion, if not thousands of parts per billion'?"

"Absolutely."

Then that is what we will use. That's it. It doesn't have to be an exact number, like twenty-seven parts per billion.

"It's not rocket science here, is it, Ana?" I quipped.

Given his professorial ways, I wasn't sure how Dr. Howard would come across in a courtroom, but I was positive he knew his field of study, and that the jurors would absolutely recognize his expertise.

Alan Care had definitely brought me to the right guy.

After the near debacle in deposition, I spent days helping Dr. Howard prepare for trial, convincing him to drop the word "possibility" from his vocabulary. I had to really beat the hell out of him to convert his scientific thought process to a legal one, because "reliability" is used differently by scientists than by those in the legal system. Scientists believe that 95 percent or more reliability is necessary to claim something is "probable." In the courtroom, we need only more than 50 percent reliability to claim something is probable.

"Don't use the word 'possibility' around me, you got it?" I'd say.

"Well, possible is possible," he'd reply.

"'Possible' doesn't exist anymore if it's greater than fifty percent!" I'd say.

In law, when you tip the scales, a thing becomes *probable*. Factual statements are based on probability or lack of probability—something either is or isn't. In the courtroom, it's really that simple. There is no gray.

In many ways, preparing Dr. Howard was like prepping an actor for a leading role, except he wasn't making up facts. He was merely learning how to present them in a legal setting.

Yeah, I knew I was getting caught up in vernacular, but in the courtroom, vernacular matters, and often it can make or break a case. And in the Castillo case, I knew DuPont would be all over any potential weakness we had, so I didn't want to hear that fucking word come out of his mouth—ever.

I bent down, got eyeball to eyeball, and said, "Your only choice of words in the courtroom are 'It's probable' or 'It's not probable.' That's it. Am I clear, Dr. Howard? Don't fucking say 'possible,' Doc. Do you understand what I'm telling you? Do you?"

I felt bad browbeating the guy into submission, but it had to be done. I couldn't allow his use of scientific terminology in a legal setting to control the outcome. I needed him to understand that he was no longer living in the scientific world. He was a scientist entering a court of law.

Dr. Howard's testimony was absolutely critical, because as my lead scientist, his testimony was the glue that held all the other scientific evidence together, which made him the captain of our team. If he slipped up, even once, whether in his deposition or testimony, we were done. Therefore, I ended up meeting with him a lot, talking through every possible scenario that might come up both in our favor and against us.

# 10

I WILL ENDURE TO BE BURNED, TO BE BOUND,
TO BE BEATEN, AND TO BE KILLED BY THE SWORD.
—*The gladiator's oath, as cited by Petronius (*Satyricon, *117).*

As THE CASTILLO-vs-DuPONT trial date drew closer, I began to feel very much like a gladiator preparing for combat. By definition, a gladiator was an armed combatant who entertained audiences in the Roman Republic and Roman Empire through violent confrontations with other gladiators, wild animals, and condemned criminals. Some gladiators were volunteers who risked their lives and their legal and social standing by appearing in the arena. Most were despised as slaves, schooled under harsh conditions, socially marginalized, and segregated even in death. Irrespective of their origin, gladiators offered spectators an example of Rome's martial ethics, and, in fighting or dying well, they could inspire admiration and rise to popular acclaim.

All gladiators trained like elite athletes, as though their lives depended on the outcome of their matches—because they did. They'd enter the arena or coliseum willing to die each time they faced a new opponent. If they survived, they were paid. If they lived three to five years doing battle, they were freed of their slave status.

When one of the opponents in a contest was wounded, the crowd would typically shout "*habet, hoc habet*," meaning "He has had it." An opponent who felt he was defeated would raise his left hand with his index finger extended in a request for mercy. It is not clear how the vote of life or death for the defeated opponent was decided, though it may have involved a gesture with the thumb by the game's presiding emperor or senator, whose judgment was often swayed by the rousing emotion of the audience.

If the decision was for death, the defeated opponent would ceremoniously grasp the thigh of his conqueror, who would slay the loser by stabbing his sword into his neck. The dead body was then removed by costumed attendants, one dressed as the ferryman Charon, the other as Mercury. Charon struck the dead body with a hammer, and Mercury poked the body with a hot iron disguised as a wand to ensure that the loser was dead. The winner would receive a symbol of his victory, such as a golden bowl, crown, or coin, along with a palm leaf.

It was a gruesome, gory sport predicated on pure bravery and bravado. Perhaps that's where the saying "No guts, no glory" stems from.

Only an arrogant or inexperienced fighter would enter the ring without knowing his opponent—how he fights, his technique, his weaknesses and strengths. This is true for any opponent in any sport. Sun Tzu said, "If you know the enemy and know yourself, you need not fear the results of a hundred battles." While I had spent nearly three years in discovery, I'd had very little interaction with the lawyers I'd be facing in the courtroom. I knew DuPont was bringing in some big guns for this trial. In addition to their in-house counsel, they hired Shook, Hardy & Bacon, a large international law firm with offices in Miami; Kirkland & Ellis to focus on appellate issues; and lead trial counsel from Glynn, Cella & Lange, a distinguished firm based in Walnut Creek, California, that specialized in these types of cases. The attorney assigned to the case from the lattermost firm was a gentleman by the name of Clement "Clem" Glynn. Clem had represented clients in a wide variety of complex litigation matters, including product liability, toxic torts, business torts, employment, real estate, intellectual property, commercial disputes, oil and gas, eminent domain, and other areas, including appellate practice. Much of his practice was focused on the defense side, but he had also successfully represented plaintiffs on many occasions. DuPont brought in Clem because they thought he was the best trial lawyer in the nation for defending in a trial like this.

Pine Island Farms hired separate counsel, going with Gaebe, Murphy & Mullen, a local firm out of Coral Gables. Founding partner Greg Gaebe was the lead attorney, and David Kleinberg was his associate. At any given time during trial, the two defendants would have at least ten attorneys in court against me and my appellate counsel.

The defendants broke the case down into two major areas: the exposure to the chemical and the science of the chemical. Pine Island was responsible for defending the exposure to the chemical, and DuPont was responsible for defending the science of the chemical. DuPont took on the science because they didn't think anyone else was smart enough to answer the scientific queries. After all, that's what DuPont does. In taking this approach, they had Gaebe's firm answer the requests for admissions, which, of course, gave us the answers we had been hoping for when we got to the courtroom. I didn't believe for a moment that DuPont's lawyers had any idea what answers Gaebe had submitted to our requests for admissions before they were delivered.

DuPont focused completely on the science, which was a lot more work than the exposure case. There were hundreds of studies that didn't matter much. The two most significant studies, the ones that made a difference in the courtroom, were the critical studies I found in the Delaware document depository—Staples I and Staples II. Naturally, there were others that helped, but those two studies were my whistleblowers. The fact that DuPont had fixed their own studies wouldn't win the case for us, but it was a sexy-enough point to create some doubt in the jury's minds about who we were dealing with and the nature of the science behind Benlate. Even so, we still had to prove that Donna's exposure at the time of her pregnancy was equally culpable.

This was my reason for bringing in thirteen different experts. Often lawyers will argue in generalities, citing "generally accepted science." This wasn't one of those cases. Given the complexity of the case, there wasn't a single person who could knowledgeably talk about *everything* we needed to prove in our case. For this reason, I sought individual experts to testify specifically and perfectly about what they knew best.

I had no room for opposing counsel to dispute such important details as the dermal transmission rate of the chemical in question. I couldn't let the other side argue that the half-life was not forty-five minutes, because it was. I couldn't let the other side suggest that people don't have three to four liters of blood in their bodies, because they do. I couldn't let the other side argue that the placenta doesn't absorb everything we consume or come into contact with through our skin, because there is no question that it does. I couldn't let the other side dispute which stage the eyes develop during gestation. And I certainly couldn't let them refute the fact that the brain is the most sensitive part of the developing embryo, or that it can be affected in a low-dose environment. I needed witnesses who could unequivocally present the facts and shut down any falsehoods if and when they came up.

With the exception of some in vitro studies that DuPont had performed themselves, the bulk of the studies hadn't been carried out on humans. As I mentioned earlier, we knew for sure that 80 percent of the time, a test conducted on a rat yields the same result as it would if the test were performed on a human. The law should probably allow that to be enough evidence to put in front of a jury, but it's not always that simple. And this is what made Dr. Howard so vital to our case. His testimony would have to convince the jury of just how small a chemical dose was needed to impact the embryo's cell development based on the science we had. He was the witness who could most easily and effectively explain, based on the level of Benlate one is exposed to, how much of the chemical would get through the skin, how much would then get into the bloodstream, and how much would pass through the placenta and ultimately to the embryo as a result. That link was the difference between winning and losing this case.

The bottom line was this: although the animal studies that resulted in eye malformations were very attention-grabbing, they clearly were not enough on their own for us to win, or even get to a jury. The animal studies showed "biological plausibility," which means, in many situations, when you get a result in an animal, you will get the same result in a human. We needed those studies, but we also needed additional science that tracked the chemical through the skin to the blood, through the blood to the placenta, and through the placenta to the embryo, into the embryo and into the cells.

# 11

My ALARM CLOCK went off at 4:30 a.m. every single day. I was living a no-frills lifestyle in my Coconut Grove apartment. By this time, I was making millions of dollars a year and was living like a guy making $40,000—well beneath my means. I didn't have time to enjoy the fruits of my labor, let alone the desire to indulge myself beyond enjoying the company of a beautiful woman every now and then. My days were long, and my stress levels were exceedingly high. Sleep had become a luxury I could no longer afford. I was out the front door and hitting the pavement hard by 5:00 a.m. to run my six miles. I'd jump in the pool at my complex afterward, then take a quick shower and head off to work again.

The trial was nearly two weeks away, and all systems were in overdrive. My relationship with Marjorie had been fizzling out for a while—at least, it had been for me. Maybe she was holding on to hope, but I had started dating other women. There was one lady I really liked. I had met her at the beginning of the year, and enjoyed the fact that she wasn't connected to my work. When we went out, it was a complete and total disconnect from everything that pulled at me, which was an escape I very much needed.

I had been struggling with telling Marjorie things were totally over. I knew she would take the news hard, but I wanted to be straight with her. I didn't want to be hiding something from someone I cared about and worked with so closely.

A couple of my buddies thought I was nuts for rattling the cage so close to the trial. They suggested that I wait until after the case ended to break the news to her, but it didn't feel right to me. I knew our relationship wasn't going any further, and I didn't want her life to be on hold. I called her on a Sunday morning eight days before the trial was set to start and told her it was over. At first I thought she took the news as well as could be expected. I knew she wouldn't be happy about it, but once we hung up I thought it had gone much better than I had anticipated. We had left things professional. Or so I thought.

That same day, I expected to meet Marjorie at the office around 11:00 a.m. to go through evidence and prepare for the trial. She wasn't there when I arrived, which was unusual. Ten minutes later, I called her cell phone. It went right to her voice mail. I called her a few more times without reaching her before I began to worry. This wasn't like her at all. She wouldn't just fail to show up—not now, not this close to the trial.

Out of concern, I finally reached out to her mother, who told me Marjorie was in Charter Hospital, though she wouldn't tell me why. She said she thought she'd be okay in time, but she didn't expect to return to work for a while—certainly not for the trial. This was very bad news.

I hung up the phone and sat in my office for hours, doing nothing but staring at the walls. I went into a funk wondering what had happened and what I could have done to change the outcome. I also questioned what I would do in the courtroom without Marjorie. She had been with me every step of the way for three years. She understood this case very well. She knew every witness, each piece of evidence we had sought together, every scientific theory, and so on. I thought about Johnny Castillo, the case, and all the changes in my life since Donna and Juan first walked through my door. So many things were different—including me.

Four hours passed by in what felt like only a few minutes.

Strangely, I didn't run to Marjorie. I didn't rush to be by her side. Her mother made it painfully clear that she didn't want me there anyway. She blamed me for what happened to her daughter, which made me feel horrible. I hadn't anticipated this. I surely didn't see this type of reaction coming. How could I?

I defended myself in my mind, recalling how I was always honest with Marjorie about my intentions. I never promised her more than I was willing to deliver in our relationship. Even when I finally filed for divorce from Diane, I told Marjorie not to see that as something I was doing for her.

We'd spent several years together—good years. As I sat and thought about those fun times, I couldn't help but take my share of responsibility for what had happened. And still, I didn't feel guilty. Not for any of it.

I didn't realize how fragile she had been throughout our relationship or in the time leading up to its ending, but at the same time I was extremely upset that she would cast aside the Castillos just days before trial. She put her personal relationship over the Castillos and their heart-wrenching situation. It was clear that she was aware I was relying on her as a critical component in the presentation of the case. Frankly, I hadn't expected her to act so selfishly.

"I really fucked up this time," I thought as I sat staring at the four walls of my office, which now felt as if they were closing in on me. Perhaps I should have kept my dick in my pants and never gotten involved with someone I worked with in the first place. Then none of this would have happened.

I knew it was stupid to be sitting there feeling so low. It wouldn't change the outcome. Besides, I didn't have the time right now to get caught up in thinking about it further. I either had to man up and fig-ure out a way to handle the case myself or find someone to assist me in the courtroom. I'd have to take each day as it came until I could work it out. It would take everything I had to pull off this Herculean feat all on my own, but what choice did I have? I wasn't about to let the Cas-tillos down. I was suddenly overcome with a rush of adrenaline and felt a little like Rocky Balboa, so to speak. There was no doubt I was the underdog, yet everything inside me told me I could win this fight.

My mind went into overdrive, and I immediately adjusted my game plan.

I brought in a friend and appellate attorney who I had known for several years named Liz Russo, who thankfully was available on such short notice. I promised her $100,000 to assist me at trial, on the condition that we win. She wasn't nearly as familiar with the case as Marjorie, but she was certainly capable of sitting next to me through-out the trial and doing research and filing various motions. Liz was a very bright attorney. Nevertheless, this was a difficult case, which would make it hard for her to jump right in and be immediately use-ful. She did, however, become my security blanket. She was someone I could bounce ideas and theories off of and get intelligent answers from. DuPont had an army—a legion of lawyers—and I had a tribe of two, one of whom was new to the case. That pretty much made me a one-man show.

The timing of Marjorie's leaving couldn't have been worse, on a lot of levels. As if that didn't add enough stress to an already pres-sured situation, my longtime secretary, Lisa, whom I had also come to heavily rely on, suddenly gave me notice that she, too, was leaving the firm a week before the start of trial. My entire world was suddenly turned upside down. Of course I did my level best without her, but it was tough. There's a rhythm that develops between a lawyer and his assistant, especially with someone like Lisa, who had been with me since October 1993. When lawyers are in trial, especially on long cases like this one, they rely on their secretaries to keep the rest of their life together. Now here I was in court with no experienced associate or secretary, I had a divorce pending, and of course I had Limogate to contend with!

The outcome of the Castillo case would have widespread implications, because Benlate had also allegedly caused similar deformities in a number of other infants in England, Scotland, Australia, and New Zealand. Besides benefiting these children, a verdict for my client could help ensure that pesticide and other chemical manufacturers would take more precautions to prevent their products from causing further harm to an unsuspecting public.

All eyes would be on the trial, as it was set to air on the newly formed Court TV network (now known as truTV). The year before, the fledgling network made Johnny Cochran a household name when it broadcast the O. J. Simpson trial. And now Court TV wanted to show this trial in its entirety. I knew this was a huge opportunity to show the world what DuPont had done to Donna Castillo's son. I was also aware that this had the potential to turn me into a household name, because no lawyer had ever won a verdict in a birth defect case against a chemical company anywhere in the world. This was more than an underdog squaring off with a giant; this was a modern-day showdown between corporate America and an innocent bystander who could have been any one of us—and everyone watching around the globe knew it. My obligation and duty was to prove this to the jury as well as show just how badly the Castillos had been wronged by DuPont on that fateful day. No one should have to unknowingly live with these consequences.

I got out of bed at 4:30 a.m. as usual on the morning of April 29, 1996, just as I had every other morning for the prior six months—only this wasn't a usual morning at all. It was day one of the Castillo trial. The trial was originally supposed to start the week before, but opposing counsel from the DuPont side asked for a continuance after one of their attorneys tragically lost his six-year-old child in a drowning accident. I told them to take whatever time they needed.

Another week wasn't going to make a difference. I assured them I wouldn't file an objection, even though I had already booked and scheduled witnesses from four countries.

"Please pass my condolences on to the family," I said. And I meant it. After all, we may be foes in the courtroom, but we were all family—men and women first and foremost.

I awoke on the morning of our initial day in court with a burst of energy, ready for my regular morning run. I clocked six miles, took a swim, and was in my car by 7:30 a.m. to arrive at the courthouse well before 8:30. I popped Bruce Springsteen's *Born to Run* into the CD player and turned up the volume as loud as it would go. I banged my left hand on the burled-wood steering wheel and shifted gears with my right. When I pulled into the parking lot of the courthouse, I decided to park my Porsche out of plain sight. Something told me I didn't want anyone—especially a potential member of the jury—to know I drove a car like this while trying a case about such a sensitive issue. I was hyper-conscientious about not offending anyone on our jury. This would become my regular morning routine throughout the trial.

I entered the courtroom with so much energy and vigor that I'm sure opposing counsel questioned the source. I didn't give a fuck. Let them think they were dealing with a hungry pit bull. I wasn't there to make friends. I was there to win.

The first order of business on the docket that morning was what is known in Florida as a Frye hearing. Federal and state courts require a minimum threshold of reliability and acceptance in the scientific community of the medical and scientific evidence to be admitted at trial. In Florida and some other states, the courts adhere to what is known as the Frye standard. Most federal and other state courts follow the Daubert standard, which is very similar to Frye. While forensic pathologists are seldom, if ever, requested to participate in such hearings, their toxicological and basic scientific colleagues often must, because they are more involved in research, methodology and technical procedures. During these proceedings, the proponent has to prove general acceptance of the methodology to be used in trial. The judge determines whether the proponent has met that burden. If the science proposed meets that burden, then the jury can consider it as evidence in the case.

DuPont's strategy from the start was to take all the evidence we submitted in the pretrial hearings, including the same evidence they submitted to the EPA, and claim it was all "junk science." They wanted the judge to say the science wasn't reliable or generally accepted in the mainstream scientific community and therefore shouldn't be allowed.

My chief complaint against DuPont was that they were claiming the exact same science they submitted to the EPA to get their product licensed was now junk science simply because I was trying to use it against them. They couldn't have it both ways. Why the hell should they be allowed to submit scientific studies (many of them self-conducted!) to the EPA to get permission to sell their chemical products to the public, and then also be allowed to turn around and call it junk science when someone from the public sues them over the harm their lethal fungicide caused? Someday this needs to be corrected. We need a federal statute that makes anything submitted to a governmental agency such as the EPA or FDA for licensing purposes admissible in a court of law, especially when scoundrels like DuPont get sued by someone like Donna Castillo. They can still call it junk science if they like, but they will have to do so directly to a jury, and they'll also have to explain to that same jury why they chose to submit junk science to the EPA or FDA in the first place.

This notion of junk science became a central theme of the trial, as it was the core of DuPont's defense. I didn't know it at the time, but this case would become the prevailing standard for years to come in the state of Florida for what type of science is or is not admissible in court. As a lawyer, I found it so unfair to the public that DuPont took such a warped and contrary position on science only when it suited their needs. The prospect of knocking out DuPont on this matter would mean a victory for us right from the start. It would be like shooting the king in the head. And from their point of view, taking out my key witness—Dr. Howard—would be like doing the same thing.

We clearly met the Frye standard and proved the general acceptance of the underlying scientific principles and procedures. DuPont, though, raised four points in the motion that we were in front of the judge to prove pursuant to Frye.

First, they claimed Dr. Howard was not a teratologist. Second, they claimed Dr. Howard's opinion was not based on any epidemiological studies. Third, they claimed Dr. Howard's use of in vitro studies (conducted by Dr. Dick Van Velzen, whom Dr. Howard had commissioned) was not acceptable. And finally they claimed Dr. Howard could not rule out alternative causes of birth defects.

In addition to those four specific attacks on Dr. Howard, DuPont also called into question and collaterally attacked the validity of Dr. Van Velzen's in vitro studies by assailing his character. Dr. Van Velzen comes from Holland and practices medicine in several countries, each of which has different rules and standards. For instance, Dr. Van Velzen had a habit of keeping preserved miscarried fetuses and embryos in his office for research purposes. In the United States, by law, you are not allowed to keep or preserve embryos and fetuses in this manner. As a result, DuPont launched a public relations smear campaign against Dr. Van Velzen, even referring to him as Dr. Frankenstein in one newspaper article. In reality, Dr. Van Velzen had an off-the-chart IQ score and was one of the most brilliant scientists on the planet, even if he wasn't the most personable individual around. Nothing ever came of DuPont's attack on Dr. Van Velzen, although, as usual, we expended a lot of effort and endured a lot of stress in protecting him, because his in vitro tests were a critical element of our case. There was no doubt his tests were performed in accordance with sound and proper scientific procedures. In fact, his methodology was precisely the same methodology DuPont used in its own in vitro tests.

Coming into the Frye hearing, we had taken the deposition of each and every expert, including Dr. Robert Brent, the supposed "King of Teratology." Dr. Brent was considered the best expert witness money could buy at the time. In his sworn testimony, he said he found several flaws in our case, including:

- That this case did not rule out genetics as a cause of John Castillo's condition before determining that another cause was probable;
- That the findings of the in vitro testing referred to in this case were not generally accepted in the scientific community (even though DuPont had conducted the tests itself!);
- That this case did not involve multiple malformations (it was DuPont's contention that when embryonic cells are exposed to toxic substances, they are likely to produce multiple malformations—unlike Johnny's single malformation, microphthalmia);
- That there were no epidemiological studies done; and
- That there was a lack of adequate evidence from animal studies.

Essentially, with the type of malformation Johnny Castillo was born with, there were two general potential causes: either genetics or environment. According to one of DuPont's star witnesses, teratologist Dr. Lewis Holmes, 70 percent of microphthalmia cases are genetic, 15 percent are environmental, and 15 percent are due to unknown causes.

Yet despite these statistics, every genetic test known to mankind, including a karyotype test, had been performed on Johnny Castillo, and the results were now indisputable. No test indicated genetics as the cause of his microphthalmia. In this regard, DuPont was left with nothing but pure speculation. Even the geneticist for the defense went so far as to testify that perhaps someday there might be a test to prove there could be a genetic cause in this type of case, but as of then, it did not exist.

This brought me to the grouping of potential environmental causes of microphthalmia that appeared on a list DuPont filed, including such teratogens as benomyl, rubella, and vitamin K, among others. But as mentioned earlier, in assessing all the environmental causes out there in the world, DuPont's expert witnesses had unwittingly ruled out all of them at deposition, and were therefore stuck with having to take those same positions at trial.

With all other potential environmental causes discounted by the opposition's own denials during the discovery process, I next placed the focus on Benlate. I already had Donna's testimony about her exposure to the spray. I had the DuPont rat studies, which proved it was a teratogen in rats. I had the outside studies that were conducted at the University of California and other places, which showed that benomyl and Benlate were both teratogens in rats. I had DuPont's skin transmission studies. I had in vitro tests that showed cell death—known as apoptosis—occurring at such small amounts as twenty-two parts per billion. I even had studies that showed neurite retraction (preventing cells from communicating) occurring at three parts per billion. All of the in vitro studies were admitted into evidence as both generally accepted and relevant. General acceptance and relevance were very easy to prove, since DuPont itself, along with literally every major drug manufacturer, uses the exact same type of tests.

What was really in question was the alleged need for epidemiology where none had previously existed. When drugs are being tested, epidemiological studies make sense, because you know who is taking the drug and who is not. You can give it to humans and study the impact by following the population. In a case like the Castillos', such a study was not possible. Pregnant women who were exposed to Benlate between seven and ten weeks into their pregnancies are very rare and extremely hard to find, as are children born with Johnny's condition—statistics show only 1 in 10,000 have it. Therefore, testing this type of chemical exposure is not only difficult but also dangerous to pregnant women, and ethically impermissible.

There was a textbook that DuPont expert Dr. Holmes agreed was authoritative. It laid out the scheme and interplay between epidemiology and animal studies, taking those two things into account and dividing them into two categories: definitive evidence and adequate evidence. Under the definitive evidence category, the textbook stated that if you were going to definitively prove developmental toxicity, you needed to have sufficient epidemiological studies from a scientific community that found a cause-and-effect relationship. To definitively prove there was no apparent effect, you needed epidemiological studies that had sufficient power. You also have to look at a variety of developmental end points. The only study of any significance to this case that we were able to uncover was an Italian study that satisfied neither point: it did not have sufficient power, and did not look at multiple end points.

DuPont had claimed that Johnny Castillo should have had more than one malformation. However, in every microphthalmia rat study we found, the majority of rats had only one malformation, not multiple malformations.

Dr. Brent's position regarding adequate evidence for potential human developmental toxicity required at least one well-executed animal study showing developmental toxicity, or strong suggestive evidence from epidemiological studies. Of course, in this case there were multiple well-executed animal studies, such as the University of California study. In fact, Dr. Staples himself, and other doctors in this case for the defense, had said the methodology of those studies was proper and that the tests were well conducted.

I was about to make my final plea to the court on behalf of Dr. Howard and his qualifications as a teratologist when I was interrupted by opposing counsel. Brian Cella was in the courtroom that morning along with Clem Glynn, both representing DuPont. Cella was incensed by my representation of Dr. Howard's credentials, which had been in question by the defense from the moment I introduced him as a witness. My contention was that during his deposition, Dr. Brent— DuPont's own witness—testified under oath that Dr. Howard was qualified to be a witness. Cella said, "Your Honor, Dr. Howard is *not* qualified. Would you like me to make clear once again our position?"

I asked the judge if I could read from Dr. Brent's deposition to remind counsel of what their own witness had said. The question had been "So you believe he is qualified; you just disagree with his opinion?"

"The answer from their expert witness, Your Honor: 'He's qualified and wrong.'"

Cella had a different point of view. He began reading from his deposition: "Dr. Brent, in your opinion, is Dr. Howard a qualified teratologist?"

"He's not a teratologist."

"And teratology is the specific discipline that studies birth defects as induced by environmental agents?"

"Among other things, yes; many of us are also geneticists as well. But certainly teratology is the study of environmental causes of birth defects in both animals and humans."

"Looking at the substance of his other opinions, you feel that he is not qualified to give these types of opinions?"

"I really try not to judge other experts. That is for the jury and the judge to decide. He certainly has had very little experience in the field of teratology, and this is not his field of expertise . . ."

Dr. Howard was known as a developmental toxicologist. A teratologist is a physician of almost any specialty who looks at birth defects. That could include pediatricians, pathologists, or any other type of medical professional, because there is no special training for teratology. That fact came from the King of Teratology himself.

Cella was getting pissed at my use of the term "King of Teratology."

"Your Honor, may I make a personal observation?" he asked.

"No. I don't think so," Judge Donner said.

"It's the reference to the King of Teratology, Your Honor . . ."

"Excuse me?" The judge wasn't happy that Cella had continued with his "observation."

"Okay, I'm sorry," Cella quickly acquiesced.

"Mr. Cella, just let Mr. Ferraro finish. Every statement he makes, there is no question in my mind and heart that you disagree. So I'll keep that in my heart as he's speaking. Then, when it's your turn, you'll tell me why you think he's wrong."

I actually didn't believe Dr. Brent was the King of Teratology any more than Cella did, but they had stated it in court, and I used the term in jest. After all, he was the self-proclaimed king in his own deposition, given under oath.

# 12

WHEN WE HAD finished with the Frye hearing, it was time to select the jury for trial. Having a good jury can make or break a case, especially a case like this. What I look for in a prospective juror is fairly simple: I want people who are open-minded and fair. I don't necessarily look for people with biases in our favor, although I will quickly exclude those with biases against us. The problem with most people is that sometimes they don't recognize they have a bias one way or the other. For instance, if your father worked as a scientist at a major pharmaceutical company, you may have trouble ruling against a pharmaceutical company despite seeing yourself as a very fair and reasonable person. Consciously or not, the fact that your dad was a scientist for such a company affects the lens through which you look at certain things. In a case like this, I didn't want members of the jury who were inadvertently biased for or against the government, corporations, or certain types of people. Even though sympathy is not supposed to play a part in a trial, both sides tend to look for jurors who are capable of or already have some sympathy toward their cause. Over the years, a good lawyer learns to operate on strong gut instincts, and that's always been my best approach when selecting a jury.

The first thing that happens during the jury selection process for a trial like ours is the court distributes a series of questions (usually in the form of a written questionnaire) to weed out people who truly cannot serve due to physical limitations, language barriers, or irresolvable family conflicts, among other legitimate reasons. Then, the judge calls smaller groups of prospective jurors to the jury box for individual questioning by the attorneys (and often by the judge, too). This is called "voir dire," which comes from an Old French term meaning "to speak the truth." During voir dire, the attorneys scrutinize each prospective juror to try to determine whether he or she would be sympathetic to one side or the other. That is one purpose of voir dire.

Another purpose of voir dire, and the one that serves the public interest in fair trials, is to determine whether a prospective juror harbors any biases that would prevent him or her from being impartial. Both the criminal and civil law systems in the United States depend upon impartial juries to hear cases in order to ensure fair trials. A defendant in a criminal case has a constitutional right to a fair trial. After questioning prospective jurors, each side's attorneys may challenge certain jurors using two types of challenges: a "for-cause" challenge and a "peremptory" challenge.

Each attorney has an unlimited number of for-cause challenges, which are, as the term suggests, based on a specified reason or "cause" to challenge the prospective juror. Generally a prospective juror may be challenged for cause because of:

- exposure to pretrial publicity about the case
- a connection with a party, an attorney, the judge, or a witness in the case
- a religious prohibition against imposing a sentence or otherwise fulfilling his or her role
- a gender, race, or other bias

When an attorney wants to challenge a juror for cause, she must state to the court the reason for that challenge. Even though the number of such challenges is unlimited, attorneys do not generally exercise very many (and frequently none at all) because of the difficulty of accusing a prospective juror of bias or incompetency to serve. The remaining jurors may resent the attorney for making a for-cause challenge, and the judge may even refuse to excuse the juror (if he or she is not persuaded that cause exists), which might harm the attorney's client more than just keeping the person on the panel in the first place.

A "peremptory" challenge is one that is made without having to state a reason. Because the attorneys for each party may make peremptory challenges without justifying them, court rules limit the number of peremptory challenges to a handful for each side. Typically, each side is allowed three peremptory challenges in a civil case. Although no reason need be given for exercising a peremptory challenge, certain reasons (such as race) are prohibited.

Before trial, attorneys for each side may turn to certain research and survey tools to test how sympathetic the jury pool in their area would be to their client's case. Some lawyers hire jury consultants, who may have detailed demographic information useful in creating a strong prospective jury pool. These consultants are often trained in areas like psychology and sociology. They also frequently attend voir dire and advise the attorney who hired them during that process. As expected, DuPont came in with a dream team of consultants to help them pick a favorable jury. I've used a consultant only one time in my career, and frankly didn't find it very helpful. After all, I'm the lawyer; I'm the guy who has to win the credibility war with the jury. No one knows me better than myself. Therefore, for this trial I chose to do it the way I usually do—without consultants, relying on my gut instincts.

In some cases, attorneys use focus groups composed of randomly selected people to see how they respond to certain portions of their case. Other lawyers conduct mock trials, presenting their cases to colleagues for insight and feedback on how jurors might respond to their presentation of evidence and their closing arguments, which is what DuPont did.

Some of these tools are very expensive, which means only a party with money can take advantage of them. This is but one of the many subtle reasons that the playing field in both civil and criminal trials is not always level.

During our voir dire process, one wiseass prospective juror actually asked me, in front of all the other prospective jurors, how much money I would make on this case. For a moment I was dumbfounded. I didn't know how to answer. I paused, hoping the judge would jump in. She didn't. Then I simply said, "Our contract is governed by the Florida Bar and is in accordance with their rules, and that is how we are compensated. Understand, sir, we don't get paid a dime if we lose." Saying this avoided telling him that we had the right to take up to one third of what got collected on a winning jury verdict or settlement, but I thought it was more important to emphasize how much risk was involved for us, as it inferred how much we believed in our case.

After a week of voir dire, we were able to settle on six jurors and a couple of alternates out of the sixty original candidates brought in. This was *such* a big case, destined to get a lot of attention, and the judge wanted to make sure we had a wide-enough selection of people to choose from. We focused on the first group of twenty, figuring we'd be able to find our jurors among them. The worst-case scenario in any jury trial is to land someone who doesn't want to be there. Sure enough, I quickly saw that this was the situation with one of the jurors who was picked. He was a real estate agent who was bitter about being tied up in a courtroom for up to six weeks instead of being out selling homes and making money. He was very antagonistic, rude, and, frankly, not very bright. Unfortunately, we were out of peremptory challenges, so my hands were tied. Our only chance to get him kicked off the jury would be a for-cause challenge.

The juror made it clear from the very start that he didn't want to be there, but he never articulated it in a way that warranted ousting him.

That was too bad for everyone, but mostly for us. I wish the judge had intervened and booted him off the case, as it was clear he was angry from the beginning. Judge Donner certainly had the discretion to do so.

This particular juror was too dumb to realize that if he really wanted out, he simply had to show that being there caused him hardship, and the judge would surely have let him go. Instead, the idiot sat there and watched as roughly a dozen other jurors before him got excused for cause. He just wasn't observant enough to figure out the magic words that would have gotten him released, too.

Jurors like this never blame the defense for being there; they always blame it on the plaintiffs, because we're the ones who filed the case. In this juror's mind, if we hadn't filed the case, he wouldn't be sitting in a courtroom losing income. We did that to him. The longer a case lingers, the angrier and more frustrated someone like this juror gets. I'd seen this type of setup too many times, and I knew it wouldn't work in our favor. If he had to sit there and bust balls, it would be mine he'd go after.

In the end, although we mostly liked the jury that was selected, we were stuck with that one bad juror, and we knew it.

# 13

I ARRIVED AT the Dade County Courthouse early on the morning of May 13, 1996. The jury had finally been selected, and it was game on. I was pumped from my morning run, testosterone raging through my veins. I was full of positive energy and ready to take on the world. I loved the challenge of getting to this place, although there was certainly a bigger and greater mountain to conquer. I truly welcomed the tests that still lay ahead. Up until this point, all I did was eat, drink, and breathe this case. I felt programmed to win, like a Navy SEAL going into Desert Storm. I wasn't thinking about anything on this day other than getting the job done.

One of the jurors was running late because of a terrible accident on I-395. She was about ten blocks away, heading in the direction of the beach and keeping the court apprised of her location. This would mean a late start, which wasn't helping the Castillos' already frayed nerves. I did my best to keep their anxieties in check while also maintaining my own focus. Donna was particularly nervous, because she was acutely aware of my intention to put her on the stand as our first witness.

Aside from the fact that I genuinely believed starting the case with her story was the best thing to do, I knew that putting Donna on first would also get her past the part she dreaded the most—facing a bunch of brutally tough lawyers such as Gaebe and Glynn. She had never testified in a trial, let alone set foot in a courtroom, in her entire life. Under the best of circumstances, this sort of thing can be daunting, even for a professional witness—which, of course, Donna was not.

Another order of business we had to address before getting started that morning involved three pieces of evidence I had submitted that Gaebe and Glynn suddenly found objectionable. The first was the day-in-the-life video I had prepared and intended to use during trial. It showed what daily life was like for little Johnny Castillo. I wanted the jury to understand how challenging it was for this young boy to live with no eyes and no hope of ever seeing. While I didn't plan to use the video in my opening statement, I certainly intended to use it at some point in the trial. This piece of evidence could be assessed later. More pressing was a four-foot-tall close-up photo of a two-month-old Johnny Castillo with his eyelids opened. DuPont and Pine Island Farms found this to be an imposing piece of evidence. They felt it gave undue emphasis and was extremely prejudicial.

While Johnny would be in the courtroom, he was now five years old. The photo depicted the boy at two months. I had no intention of putting him on the stand or allowing him to open his eyes in front of the jury. I didn't think that would be proper in this case. While an ocularist and an ophthalmologist would testify about certain treatments, there was no cause to demonstrate them in front of the jury—though the jury would need to get some idea of what would happen when Johnny underwent such treatments. The jury would also hear about prosthetics—something we hoped Johnny would receive in the future, after he was done growing. These prosthetics would give the appearance of eyeballs, and would require metal clamps and screws to help keep them in place.

Glynn and Gaebe argued that the jury could understand all this without seeing the photograph—and certainly not a photo the size of the one I submitted into evidence. They compared it to what one would find in criminal cases or accident cases in which there was no real dispute over injury.

The judge agreed with me that if the attorneys were going to analogize the evidence to those types of cases, they should note that in a criminal case, especially in a murder case, the victim is dead, and more often than not, photos of the individual are shown. The issue to be decided was, what was too gruesome to show in a courtroom? While the photo of Johnny wasn't pleasant, the judge didn't find it grisly or prejudicial, and therefore denied the defense's motion to exclude the exhibit.

This was a very good way to start the case.

The third piece of evidence Glynn and Gaebe had an issue with was a Pine Island exhibit that read, "Benlate is the only fungicide used before 11/10/89."

Their reason?

They said there was simply no evidence to support that statement.

They argued that to put up anything that suggested this would be extremely prejudicial, and no matter what they did to try to dispel that characterization would be unsuccessful. They went on to argue they didn't know who wrote that statement, even though it came from the business records of Pine Island Farms. Typically, records kept in the ordinary course of business are admissible. Furthermore, I had substantial evidence to support this statement, from the Benlate purchase records to the testimony of Lynn Chaffin. In fact, they had a time line noting when they planted tomatoes that supported this statement. Before I could continue stating why I thought this piece of evidence should be admissible, the judge denied their motion.

Score another one for the plaintiff.

At this point, Gaebe asked, "Has anyone heard from the juror we're waiting for?"

"She's ten blocks away. We're talking her in to the courthouse now. Let's take a fifteen-minute recess until she gets here. We are adjourned," said Judge Donner.

The atmosphere in the courtroom was very tense. The air was so thick you could cut it with a dull butter knife. It was well known that no chemical company had yet been held responsible for a birth defect, which made this trial even more dramatic to all of those involved. Court TV had their cameras set up and ready to begin daily coverage of the trial. I wasn't sure if anyone would watch, but I knew a positive outcome in this case could potentially impact millions of people around the world. There was a lot at stake, and that fact in and of itself certainly made for good television, especially for this up-and-coming cable channel.

"Ladies and gentlemen, in just a minute the jury will be coming in." The judge addressed the courtroom, which was packed. Everyone involved in the case from all sides was present.

"Counsel, the jury is coming in," said Ray, the judge's clerk, as the six-member panel and the alternates made their way into the courtroom.

"Will the jury please remain standing? The rest of you may be seated." Judge Donner said as the jury was sworn in.

"You have now been sworn in as the jury for this case. This is a civil case involving a disputed claim or claims among the parties. Those claims and other matters will be explained to you later. By your verdicts, you will decide the disputed issues of fact. I will decide the questions of law that arise during the trial, and before you retire to deliberate at the close of the trial, I will instruct you on the law you are to follow and apply in reaching your verdicts. In other words, it is your responsibility to determine the facts and to apply the law to those facts. The function of the jury and the function of the judge are well defined and do not overlap. This is one of the fundamental principles of our system of justice."

Judge Donner carefully laid out her expectations for everyone, making it extremely clear her patience for the theatrics that had gone on during the pretrial and Frye hearings had run thin, and she was not going to tolerate game playing from either side. She also instructed the members of the jury on what they could expect during the trial, reminding them that they were not to discuss the case among themselves or with anyone else, nor were they to permit anyone to say anything to them or in their presence about the case. Attorneys, witnesses, or any other parties associated with the case were especially off-limits until the deliberations were finished, so as to avoid the appearance of anything improper.

I could feel the anticipation building and the air in the courtroom intensifying with every word the judge spoke. I think everyone there could feel it, especially with the television cameras present and so much at stake.

Tension is an interesting quality. In some ways it's desirable in situations like this, and still I find there are always elements of the inexplicable, the poetic, and the mysterious that make it feel perfectly rational.

Sitting at the DuPont defense table were Clem Glynn, Doug Chumbley, Brian Cella, and DuPont's corporate representative, Dr. Judith Stadler. At the defense table for Pine Island Farms were Greg Gaebe and David Kleinberg, Lynn Chaffin, and Jack Wishart, who started Pine Island Farms in 1983.

Sitting with me at our table were my appellate counsel Liz Russo, my associate (of only eight months) Ana Rivero, and the Castillo family, including Donna, Juan, Adrianna, and little Johnny.

Without much fanfare or ado, Judge Donner finished her explanations and said, "At this time the attorneys will have the opportunity to make their opening statements, in which they may explain to you, the jury, the issues in the case and give you a summary of the facts they expect the evidence to show. Is the plaintiff ready to proceed to trial?"

"Yes, Your Honor," I replied.

"You may begin," she said.

I stood up from behind the walnut-brown table that would become my home base in the courtroom for the next several weeks, straightened my suit jacket, turned to the jury—then turned to John Castillo, sitting in the front row just behind Liz and Ana, and took a short pause before turning around once again to face the jury.

"Good morning, ladies and gentlemen; thank you for serving on our jury. I'm going to give you a very brief introduction. If I had only forty-five seconds to tell you about this case and what the evidence will show, this is what I would tell you.

"In 1989, Donna Castillo lived in West Kendall. On approximately September nineteenth of 1989, she became pregnant with her young son, John, who is right over there, sitting on Mr. Castillo's lap. About seven weeks into her pregnancy, she was walking by a farm in her neighborhood where they were spraying a product called Benlate. The farm is one of the defendants in the courtroom. The product is made by the other defendant.

"She was drenched with a spray of this product seven weeks into her pregnancy. The following June—June 15, 1990, to be exact—her son was born with no eyes." Ironically, Johnny was born on the exact date of my and Diane's tenth wedding anniversary. Something about that connection felt important and relevant as we began our battle. I continued with my opening, staying very much on script and being deliberate with every word.

"This particular product has been tested through the years by scientists both inside of DuPont and outside of DuPont. They have performed a number of rat studies in which they intentionally exposed pregnant rats to doses of Benlate, and in almost all of those tests, a substantial number of rat fetuses were born without eyes, just like John Castillo was.

"Now, I want to tell you a little bit about the product Benlate. Benlate was first introduced in 1968 as an experimental fungicide. During the 1970s, it was marketed under the trade name Benlate

50 DF. That is the product at issue in this courtroom. The product is used to spray strawberries, tomatoes, and a variety of other types of fruits and vegetables.

"The active ingredient in Benlate is something called benomyl. Benlate is the product name, and benomyl is the active compound. This is the active ingredient that was tested on rats.

"The product is registered with the Environmental Protection Agency of the United States. In 1977, the EPA issued what is known as Position Paper Number One on Benlate. What this means is that the EPA, as part of its process, looks at data submitted by the manufacturer of a product for review, and they rely on the manufacturer's representation of the product to decide whether it should be allowed to go on the market. Part of the reason it is done this way is that the manufacturer clearly has the most intimate knowledge about its product.

"In 1977, the EPA was concerned about skin exposure to Benlate—getting the product on one's skin, also known as dermal exposure. They were also concerned about food ingestion and inhalation of the product. As a result of those concerns, the EPA working group—a panel that looks at products—issued what is known as a "Rebuttable Presumption Against Registration" against DuPont. Their position stated specifically that the amount of benomyl to which women of childbearing age might be exposed is too high relative to the dose that has produced birth defects in animals. The birth defect being looked at is microphthalmia, along with some others. The rebuttable presumption remained in effect after 1977.

"Our evidence will show that DuPont vigorously fought the rebuttable presumption that this product was dangerous to pregnant women such as Donna Castillo, even though it remained in effect until 1979, when the EPA issued yet another position paper that proposed some sort of protection for women like Donna Castillo. This position paper suggested that while the product needn't be pulled from the market, word should be put out to the public that methods to reduce exposure, such as wearing protective masks, were necessary. And still, DuPont's opposition remained persistent and vigorous. The rebuttable presumption remained in effect until 1982.

"The reason for the lift of the rebuttable presumption in 1982, after five years, will shed light on DuPont's own methodology in its studies, as shared by their own head of toxicology, Dr. Robert Staples. Dr. Staples, who worked at DuPont, performed a rat study in 1980 at the request of the EPA, the result of which was not good for DuPont, because the low effect level at which bad results could be seen didn't get DuPont off the hook as they had hoped. Dr. Staples will explain that he did another study in 1982 that yielded a lower effect level, and it was that study that got the EPA to give DuPont a pass. However, you will hear the reasons the results were different in 1982, and why they shouldn't have been.

"In the meantime, DuPont continued to oppose alerting people like Donna Castillo because it was a competitive advantage not to do so. They didn't feel that they should have to do something competitors with products that did not contain benomyl did not have to do.

"In 1987 and 1991 at the University of California, two scientists unrelated to DuPont conducted some additional studies on the effects of benomyl to determine whether it played a role in causing microphthalmia. One scientist by the name of Hoogenboom tested benomyl at 62.5 milligrams per kilogram of body weight in order to analyze eye abnormalities, which included microphthalmia. Something very dramatic happened in this test. In Hoogenboom's study, a shocking 43 percent of all the rat fetuses that were born had eye abnormalities. In Hoogenboom's study, if the rats were given a protein-deficient diet in addition to benomyl, the rate went up to 60 percent.

"Since DuPont had conflicting results in their own studies, logically they should have done a third study after they were cleared in 1982, but they didn't. They were so happy to be off the hook that they didn't want to call more attention to a product they knew was harmful. Finally, in 1985, DuPont did conduct another study, but this time they did it on rabbits. DuPont will claim they were told to do it on rabbits, but that's garbage. As the manufacturer of a product, they can do whatever they want with regard to testing a product for safety, including more rat studies if they want to. But they didn't. They chose rabbits for a reason. The problem with rabbits is that they have what is known as a double-lined placenta, which means that, unlike in a rat, little if any of the chemical will get to the embryo or fetus in a rabbit. The human placenta is even more sensitive than a rat's, which makes using a rabbit for this study almost totally irrelevant.

"You will be hearing the word 'teratology' a lot throughout this case, and it's important to understand that it is the study of birth defects. In the United States, doctors who study birth defects can be pathologists, developmental toxicologists, and even pediatricians. As long as they look at birth defects, they are practicing teratology. There is no special training and no special degree required to call oneself a teratologist. When it comes to teratology, there will be two distinctions that come up. The battle will be between rats and humans and drugs and chemicals. DuPont will show more known teratogens in rats. There is no question about that, because you can test a lot of things on rats—such as chemicals like benomyl—but you can't test those things on humans. That has not been done since World War II. The interplay between chemicals and drugs is important, because the one area in which you get a lot of data with regard to humans is with drugs. There is no benefit to exposing humans to chemicals to see if they are teratogens. Drugs, however, have a lot of possible benefits for humans, so there can be clinical trials in which you give drugs to people to determine whether those drugs have benefits and whether there are potential downsides. That is why you will find there are more known teratogens for rats than for humans.

"Ladies and gentlemen, you will hear a lot of double-talk in this case from DuPont, because they believe rat studies are great when you are trying to get a product to market, but those same rat studies are useless and don't mean a darn thing when you try to use the studies against them."

I went on to tell the jury about the day Donna Castillo came into contact with Benlate, describing Pine Island Farms in as much detail as possible to help give them a visual picture of the field to accompany the blown-up photographs of the area I used as evidence. About one-third of the field was used to grow tomatoes, and the other two-thirds were used for strawberries.

I showed the jury a photograph of the tractor that had gotten stuck in the mud on the day that Donna was exposed. Weather records indicated that the wind was blowing out of the southeast. It had been a strong wind, between twelve and fourteen miles per hour, with gusts of up to twenty mph.

As Donna described it, the spray that drenched her was a foggy type of mist. It was odorless and had no smell or color, and was whitish on the skin. As anyone would have, she didn't think much of it at the time, though she told her husband what happened when she got home because she was soaked to the bone. It wasn't until the following June when their son was born with severe microphthalmia that they realized something had gone terribly wrong.

"This is Johnny at two months," I said as I pointed to the four-foot-tall close-up photograph of their baby.

The family had been shocked by what happened to Johnny, because there were no risk factors in their family history, and their daughter, Adrianna, who was sitting in the courtroom that morning next to Donna, had been born with two perfect, beautiful, healthy eyes.

I shared the story of John Ashton's investigative report with the jury, and of the Scottish families whose children had been affected by exposure to Benlate, as well as the documented conversations Ashton and I had both had with Lynn Chaffin, which showed the farm used Benlate in November of 1989.

I needed the jury to understand that this was going to be a complex case but that I would do my very best to help them understand and break down all of the evidence into bite-sized nuggets they could digest, especially when it came time to hear all the scientific witnesses. Above all, I needed them to see the Castillos as strong people who were making the very best of a very bad situation. They had moved from Miami to Palm Beach because John needed to be in a special school. As a result, they each had to change jobs. Johnny required constant attention. He didn't sleep like a normal person. He could go through periods when he might sleep from midnight to 2:00 a.m., or from 4:00 to 5:00 in the afternoon. Sometimes he was up all night, but it was all part of the Castillos' routine. "At the end of the day, this is the story of a little boy who will never see his mom or dad. He will never see his sister, Adrianna, and he will never get better. His eyes will never grow in; he has no chance to have his eyesight."

When I finished, I turned back to the jury and reminded them that it was their job and their duty to hear the evidence in this case and apply it to the law, and I told them I would be asking for a verdict after the close of the evidence for the plaintiffs.

"It will be in the millions of dollars," I said, knowing, hoping, and, yes, even praying they wouldn't see it any other way.

Next up was Greg Gaebe, on behalf of Pine Island Farms.

Greg's opening focused on the issues directly involving the spraying portion of the case, because that was the portion that dealt with the farmer. The three questions he posed in the courtroom that morning were:

1. Did Pine Island Farms have a spray rig at the field in question on November 1 or 2, 1989?
2. Was the tractor on the spray rig positioned in the manner described by Mrs. Castillo?
3. Was Mrs. Castillo drenched with Benlate?

Gaebe's contention was that their evidence would show the answers to all three of those questions were a resounding *no, no,* and *no.* He claimed their evidence would show that Pine Island Farms did *not have* Benlate, did *not use* Benlate, and did *not purchase* Benlate that farming season until December 19. He also stated that their evidence would show they did not use Benlate and had no reason to use Benlate on the first or second of November in that particular field. Gaebe then explained to the jury that Pine Island Farms didn't own the land they farmed—they leased it.

As I listened to his opening, all I could think was, "Who cares who owns the land?" It had no relevance to the liability in the case. What he was attempting to show was that the farm operated as a commercial farm. Their primary business was growing tomatoes on what they referred to as commercial fields. They had to plan ahead of time what would be planted in each field. As part of their everyday operations, they had several U-Pick farms, which are different from commercial fields. The primary crop of the U-Pick fields was strawberries.

This commentary about what type of field they were spraying—commercial or U-Pick—was a lame attempt to divert the jury's attention from what was important in the case. They used Benlate regardless of who was purchasing their crops.

According to Gaebe, every year at Pine Island Farms, strawberry season started in the middle or end of August. The farmers would come back and fix their equipment, getting it ready for the new season to begin. They wanted to farm through the winter so their produce would be available in the proper market conditions. To take advantage of the tropical climate in Florida, they grow fruits such as tomatoes and strawberries when they cannot be grown in other parts of the country.

To get the soil ready, a farmer has to disk the ground, which involves tilling the earth. This process also removes weeds that may have grown over the summer. Disking essentially prepares the field to be planted, and, depending on the ground height and the soil configuration (meaning how much rock, coral, or other debris is present), a farmer may have to disk the land three or more times to get it ready for the planting process.

After disking the field, the farmer will use a special piece of equipment to mark the rows. If you laid down on the ground and looked at the field, you would see that the beds are higher than the ground in between the rows, giving the land a slightly rippled appearance. Once the field has been configured in this way, the farmer fertilizes it and lays down plastic.

This process is known as laying granular fertilizer. It is called 6:12:12 to reflect the proportionate amounts of potassium, magnesium, and nitrogen the fertilizer contains. All the fields that are being prepared for planting are treated the same way and at the same time up to this stage. After the plastic is laid, methyl bromide is put down. If you've ever had your house tented, you will recognize this as a similar process, whereby the chemical seeps into the ground and sanitizes the earth, killing roundworms, insects, and other pests. After this is done, the farmer needs to wait ten days to two weeks before planting.

Tomatoes are usually the first crop to be planted, followed by strawberries at the U-Pick fields. In this case, Gaebe told the jury that tomatoes were planted in September, and they were certain that strawberries were planted at the field in question no sooner than October 25, 1989.

Gaebe's opening statement began to get very opinionated. He talked about his thoughts on the case instead of what the evidence might show. I finally got so fed up with his tactics that I objected. "Your Honor, Mr. Gaebe has been doing a lot of arguing, but we need to make sure he gets his facts right."

The judge had previously warned each of the attorneys against doing what Gaebe was doing, as she sensed this might be the way we were all going to operate. When it got to the point where she could no longer take it, she would call for a sidebar and tell us to stop arguing points. The danger in what Gaebe was doing is that it risks swaying the jury toward what you *believe* to be true instead of what the evidence actually shows. When counsel is talking about "his efforts" in discovery over certain evidence, it can potentially be very damaging.

As a result of Gaebe's long-winded approach, Judge Donner put a limit on the time he had left to finish his opening statement, which concluded with his efforts to discredit John Ashton and the call Ashton had with Chaffin.

It had been a drawn-out and draining morning, but I thought we did great, at least in comparison to Gaebe. The judge excused everyone for lunch before we returned for the opening statement from Clem Glynn.

From the moment Glynn began to speak, I knew I was watching a great lawyer. In a way, he reminded me a little of Clint Eastwood. He had presence, oozed believability, and was ruggedly polished. In many ways, he was the ideal opponent. He knew exactly how to work the courtroom—to speak to the jury and address them in a manner that is gained only through experience and expertise. He was smug and arrogant, and wasn't going to be easy to match on any level.

David had finally come eye to eye with Goliath.

"Ladies and gentleman, whatever weight you choose to give to Mrs. Castillo's description of the events that occurred, one thing is clear: she does not say and cannot say that whatever it was she felt or thinks she felt on that day was Benlate." He finessed every word, pause, and breath with deliberate intent to create doubt. Glynn's argument was to portray John's birth defect as a genetic defect, stating that the experts in this case would explain why this was the only probable cause. Worse, in my opinion, was that Glynn chose to bring up personal (make that *very* personal) history about Donna Castillo's troubled pregnancy with John. Glynn shared with the jury that Donna had had infertility problems in 1986 and went to Boston to be seen by a specialist who diagnosed her with various kinds of internal scarring in her reproductive system. He also brought up a possible miscarriage in 1987, along with her irregular period cycle and reported spontaneous abortions or miscarriages. A 1987 ultrasound revealed that she had a two-month-old fetus inside her that was dead and needed to be removed via a medical procedure. It was all very embarrassing for Donna, and very irrelevant and unnecessary.

Glynn's explanation for raising this history was that often in miscarriages there can be accidents in which people get banged around, and it's nature's way of ridding the body of a grossly defective child. According to Glynn, however, John's defect was "less gross, and Mrs. Castillo's body was able to bring him to term."

Listening to Glynn go down this trail infuriated me, and I knew it crushed my clients. It was totally irrelevant, but not something the judge would block in the opening statement because Glynn would simply say the evidence would later show it, even though it wouldn't. Therefore, I just had to live with it.

As we expected, Glynn began to discuss Benlate and the rat studies and all the reasons the DuPont studies were appropriate. He also relied on the premise that even if Benlate had been a factor, the most likely cause of Johnny's birth defect was genetic and that there would be testimony to support that probability over and over again.

This was the stance DuPont was taking. And it was enough to create doubt, that was for sure. I had my work cut out for me, but it wasn't an impossible task. It would take better evidence and witnesses that were more believable than theirs—starting with Donna Castillo.

# 14

IMMEDIATELY FOLLOWING THE conclusion of opening statements, Donna Castillo nervously took the stand. There was no recess between the opening statements and her testimony. It was definitely "game on."

I took a slow, deep breath and started off by asking Donna simple background questions about where she lived, her age, and her occupation. She explained to the jury that she worked as a preschool teacher's aide in West Palm Beach, making around five dollars an hour. She worked every day from seven thirty in the morning until two in the afternoon teaching a general preschool curriculum. Going back to teach full-time as she did when she and Juan lived in Miami simply wasn't a viable option ever since she had given birth to Johnny.

"My son needs me. I really couldn't dedicate myself in the same capacity as I could when I was a full-time teacher. Being an aide allows me to devote myself to him when I get home from school," Donna said, her voice trembling.

If she had gone back to work full-time, she would be making significantly more money—at least $30,000 a year, if not more. The financial and emotional strain on her family was obvious.

I asked Donna to share with the jury how she had discovered she was pregnant with her son. She told us she took a home pregnancy test in November 1989. She and her husband, Juan, had been trying to conceive another child and were hoping Donna was pregnant. From the moment the news was confirmed, she took excellent care of her body as most expectant mothers would, not smoking or drinking alcohol.

Baby John Castillo was born at South Miami Hospital on June 15, 1990. The Castillos were jubilant, as one might expect new parents to be. Immediately after Johnny's birth, Donna held him against her bare chest. A mother's love is indescribable at that moment of bonding when she holds her newborn in her arms for the very first time. She looked down at her son and, for a split second, thought his eyelids looked rather puffy. It never occurred to her that there could be something dreadfully wrong with his eyes.

The labor nurse took John from Donna's arms to wash him and administer the silver nitrate drops that are placed in all babies' eyes. John was crying a lot, perhaps more than normal. Certainly more than Donna recalled her daughter, Adrianna, crying when she was born.

"Is something wrong?" Donna called out.

But no one answered amid the flurry of activity in the delivery room.

It was only later that Donna and Juan would be told that their son's eyelid skin was fused shut. The nurse wasn't able to give him the drops as she normally would. She called in some specialists who congratulated the Castillos on the birth of their son, but even then, no one spoke of the horrible surprise the family was about to receive. They simply brought Donna back to the labor room to bathe her.

It was while Donna and Juan were making their way back to their private room that they encountered a neonatologist from the hospital.

He introduced himself and nonchalantly said he wasn't totally sure, but he thought maybe John had been born without eyes.

"I remember staring at this doctor in shock and then hearing my husband say, 'You mean to tell me you're saying he doesn't have any eyes?' And all I remember is seeing the doctor's mouth move without hearing any sound," Donna said as tears slowly streamed down her cheeks.

There was no family or genetic history of this type of birth defect on either Donna's or Juan's side. In fact, after John was born, both Donna and Juan had significant genetic testing done, and their results reflected perfectly normal genetic makeups for each of them. No genetic defects were present in them or anywhere in their families. While Donna had undergone fertility treatments to conceive her first child, there was no evidence that any of the fertility drugs she had taken would have caused the birth defect John was born with. Nor was there any evidence that surgeries Donna underwent prior to giving birth to her son could have led to his condition.

One of the defense's arguments was that Donna's past medical history might have been a possible cause of John's birth defect. In particular, the opposing team was aggressively going to attempt to plant seeds of doubt around Donna's fertility issues and subsequent miscarriages during the time she and Juan were trying to conceive. There was absolutely no medical evidence to prove those miscarriages, which took place two years prior to Johnny's conception, were related to his being born without eyes. No medical doctor of any sort had ever stated to Donna and Juan that there was any relationship whatsoever. This was an extremely important point to make, because despite the lack of medical viability, the defense was going to go after Donna hard on these issues in cross-examination.

Once I felt we had sufficiently covered Donna's medical history, it was time to recap that fateful day in November 1989. I set up an easel with photographs of the neighborhood Donna and Juan lived in so she could re-create the route of her walk on the day in question. The Castillos lived in an apartment complex called LeParc on SW 142 Street at the corner of SW 96th Street in West Kendall. She took walks often, usually twice a day. If her schedule allowed, she liked to go out in the morning after breakfast and again in the afternoon, sometime after lunch. Her daughter, Adrianna, was still a toddler at the time, so wherever Donna went, she was usually pushing her in a stroller.

Donna stepped out of the jury box and began using the blown-up photos and a red marker to diagram her route as she explained what happened to her on the first or second of November 1989. She said she walked down SW 96th Street with her daughter and entered a driveway into a shopping plaza. It was a beautiful day, but noticeably windy—so windy she had difficulty pushing the stroller. As she walked into the driveway and past a building next to the car wash in the plaza where there were gas pumps and a Food Spot, she felt sprinkles. At the time, she thought it was nothing more than a sun shower. Of course, that wasn't an uncommon occurrence for south Florida. So Donna kept walking, continuing to push the stroller in the direction of the building near where the gas pumps were located in the front of the plaza. It was there that she noticed a tractor across the street on 137th Avenue, where Pine Island Farms was located. At the time, 137th Avenue was just a two-lane road, so the distance from where she stood to the edge of the farm field wasn't far. The tractor was stuck in mud, very close to the road. It was idling, but the sprayer attachment was bucking and jerking. As Donna described it to the courtroom, "it had tons of a foggy, cloudy mist blowing and coming out of it."

Out of curiosity, Donna stopped to watch what was happening. The bucking and jerking continued, as did the spraying of the mist. Donna stood motionless and mesmerized. She wondered what was happening. Before she realized it, the mist began blowing toward her. She couldn't get out of the way. Her clothes and body were soaked, as though she had stood outside in the rain. Her hair, face, arms, and legs were all exposed and doused in this unknown colorless, odorless spray.

When it occurred to Donna that both she and her daughter were soaking wet, she turned around and pushed the stroller back toward the shops. She stopped under an overhang near a Pizza Hut, turned, and looked back at the tractor one last time. Spray was still spewing into the air.

Donna went home and told her husband what had happened that day. At the time, she never imagined she had been sprayed with anything dangerous. Even after her daughter became ill a week later, vomiting as if she had a terrible flu, Donna still didn't suspect they had encountered anything that would harm her unborn child. While recounting her story, Donna testified that in retrospect, she believed Adrianna's "flu" was caused by her exposure to the Benlate. This testimony infuriated Glynn and Gaebe, who both objected in the form of a motion for a mistrial, because Donna's offering of this opinion was directly contrary to an earlier ruling made by Judge Donner during the Frye hearings just one week before the trial began that Donna could not express an opinion as to the cause of Adrianna's fever. Thankfully, the judge denied their motion, though she did instruct the jury to disregard that remark.

Benlate wasn't on the Castillos' radar as a possible cause for John's condition until Donna was contacted by John Ashton. It was in April of 1993 that she first learned the mist she was sprayed with that day might have been the culprit. Ashton told Donna he was investigating a link between the fungicide Benlate and children born with microphthalmia. After three or four conversations, they were able to connect Donna's walk near Pine Island's strawberry and tomato fields on that November day with John's birth defect. Ashton had spoken to the owner of the farm, who confirmed that they had used Benlate and were spraying it during the time of Donna's pregnancy with John in November of 1989. This information was relayed to the Castillos in May of 1993. Shortly after that revelation, Donna saw a television commercial touting the health benefits of organic farming. The commercial showed a tractor with a large sprayer attachment like the one that sprayed Donna that day in 1989. She suddenly realized in horror that this must have been how she was exposed to Benlate. She talked to her husband after her conversation with Ashton and again after seeing the commercial on TV. "Juan, this has to be it," she said. "How else can you explain it?"

Although Donna Castillo was a very good and experienced school-teacher, when she brought her son home from the hospital, she had no idea what to do. She had years of experience working with children, but not with children who couldn't see. Our plan was to show the jury an eighteen-minute day-in-the-life video illustrating what the Castillos' ongoing challenges looked like. It depicted the special assistance Johnny needed and the techniques he used to eat breakfast, brush his teeth, get ready for school, navigate the stairway in his home, and overcome countless other obstacles (including bumping into walls) during his daily routine, until finally going to bed. Opposing counsel was against showing the video from the start. There was no other Florida case that had denied the use of a day-in-the-life video. The judge knew this and agreed that we should be able to show it to the jury. Just when I thought we had put the issue to bed, Doug Chumbley raised a new concern: the video showed John Castillo in the nude.

I could hardly believe what I was hearing. Chumbley made it appear as though we had filmed this five-year-old boy running around stark naked; in fact, the cameraman had shot from a distance while Donna got her son dressed in the morning. This was simply what they did every day, and comprised less than five seconds of footage. We also wanted to show that while Johnny Castillo may not have had eyes, there was nothing wrong with the rest of his body. Johnny was at his most vulnerable when he walked into walls, fell on the floor, and couldn't help himself up. It wasn't when his mother dressed him. Chumbley's argument was absurd, and the judge knew it.

Gaebe hadn't seen the video—at least, not the edited, shortened version. He had been provided the original two-hour raw footage. "Your Honor, the original version is six to eight hours long," he said.

"It's two hours, Mr. Gaebe," the judge replied.

"Well, it felt like it."

Gaebe found many parts of the two-hour footage objectionable but hadn't bothered to raise those issues until we stood in front of the judge moments before I wanted to show the video to the jury. His claim not to have seen the shortened version didn't sit well with the judge. If I had given him only the shorter version, he might have had a viable argument. But since he had seen everything in the longer one, there would be no surprises. Therefore, I would be able to use the video.

Before asking the jury to watch the footage, I wanted them to hear from Donna what it was like to suddenly be faced with raising a child with no eyes. She began by talking about the first two years of his development, which were quite different from what a typical newborn or infant would experience. As a totally blind baby, Johnny lay very still. He didn't know any world other than darkness. All his learning came through listening to sounds. With no visual contact, there can be no visual response. When Donna or Juan looked at their son, he could not look back. When they smiled at him, he could not return the smile. He didn't twine his fingers, what experts call midline fingers, or even move one hand to touch the other because he wasn't aware he had fingers or hands. Blind babies don't realize they have extensions to their bodies.

To connect with her son, Donna spent a great deal of time massaging and caressing him with lotions and creams and teaching him how to move his hands, clap them together, and open and close them; to clutch a rattle and to pick up his foot and bring it toward his mouth, as babies do; and to roll over, as well as reach all the other typical physical milestones an infant experiences. To accomplish this, she would make sounds that Johnny could recognize in order to guide him. Donna and Juan encouraged their son's movement through music and other aural clues they thought might inspire him. If blind babies aren't motivated or stimulated to move, it can result in serious developmental delays. Lying down in one position for too long can also cause infants to have a very flatly shaped head.

During the first three and a half years of Johnny's life, he couldn't sleep the whole night through. Sometimes he'd be awake all night long. Totally blind children are often unable to produce enough serotonin to sleep all night. For them, it's as if they are in a constant state of jet lag. There were many times when Johnny would wake up at 3:00 a.m., go without a nap during the day, and still not be able to fall asleep until nine or ten at night. Since he wasn't active like other children, it made sleeping very hard. The family tried to do things to encourage some physical activity. They would tie a jump rope around his waist and run with him or use a hula hoop to get him to move around, but these were all assisted activities, meaning Donna and Juan were never without their son in tow.

A blind child has no reason to want to crawl. Sighted infants' motivation is usually to move toward something they see. For a blind child to want to crawl, you must encourage that child with the sound of an object he likes to reach for, or, of course, with his mother's voice. To get him to crawl, Donna also had to help Johnny strengthen his head, chin, and neck muscles. Because sight wasn't what was guiding his movement, he had no reason to want to pick up his head. Instead, his inclination was to slide it along the carpeting in their home. It was up to Donna to teach him how to lift his head so he could actually move forward. While Donna had no special training in any of this, the Dade County Public School system did provide therapists who came to the Castillo home shortly after Johnny was born to give the family some tips on how to begin educating him. This was incredibly helpful, especially since the family was not financially able to pay for help on their own.

To help a blind child progress from crawling to walking requires a great deal of trust. It is a scary-enough thing to balance oneself without holding on to anything or anyone, but it is especially scary for a blind child. He needs to be old enough to focus his mind and understand directions—left, right, up, down—which makes learning to walk a very big deal for a blind child. At the time we were discussing his story in court, Johnny was learning to walk with the assistance of a cane, but he was struggling with it. While he was comfortable in his own environment at home, stairs, corners, and the kitchen counter were still obstacles he had to contend with on a daily basis because he would forget they were there. Walking with the aid of a guide dog was a possibility, but that couldn't happen until he was at least sixteen years old, according to a psychologist the Castillos spoke with shortly after John was born. At the time, he could feed himself only finger food, was unable to bathe himself, and couldn't go to the bathroom without assistance. He was completely dependent on his parents. He had also come to a place in his young life where he realized he was different, that he had no eyes, and that this was the reason he was always in the dark.

As a parent, Donna Castillo had struggled with guilt. She didn't ask for Johnny to have a life like this. She had a very difficult time dealing with her grief over the damage that was done to her son. She was not the same person she once was, and couldn't be the kind of parent to her daughter, Adrianna, she had hoped to be because of the demands placed on her by the family's situation. Adrianna had been through a lot, too. She had two parents who were exhausted, sleep-deprived, depressed, and grieving as they tried to deal with her brother's challenges the best they could. Donna Castillo spent the bulk of her days and nights caring for her son, worrying about his every move. She was concerned about how she was going to take care of him. She worried, too, about who would assume that caregiving role after she died someday. She was constantly focused on Johnny's needs, placing them over her own, and above the rest of the family's as well. The physical and emotional toll had been immeasurable on all of the Castillos, but Donna seemed to carry a greater burden of the sort of guilt only a mother could understand.

Donna's testimony was hard but necessary. And there was no doubt the entire courtroom was moved by her plight.

When I finished with my questions, Glynn was ready to cross-examine Donna. I was hopeful he would be refined, though I knew he, too, had a job to do. I wasn't sure Donna had it in her to meet him eye to eye. I hoped she did.

Glynn offered to give Donna a moment to compose herself before getting started. She refused, saying, "That's okay. I'm fine."

Glynn did his best to take Donna through her story of that November day and discredit every detail of her account of what had happened, from the path she walked to the blowing wind. While she had been rock solid when I asked about the events of the day, she wavered a bit when Glynn questioned her. He was trying to confuse her or the jury. Glynn drew his version of Donna's route on a map for the jury to see, which didn't quite match our map. It was close but not exact, which left some room for debate. In a courtroom, debate equals doubt. In his cross-examination, Glynn got Donna to say she stood on the shoulder of the driveway for a couple of minutes watching the tractor as it continued to spray, and then specifically asked if she was there for two or three minutes, which is how she testified earlier. Glynn persisted, asking Donna the same questions five or six times, repeating himself over and over until the judge finally called for a sidebar. She was clearly annoyed with his tactic of trying to get the witness to misspeak. She laid down the law there and then, telling Glynn that he had the right to ask each question one time and then he had to move on to the next.

Admittedly, it had been a long day, and it was getting late. In fairness to the court and the jury, she was right; Glynn's line of questioning was obnoxious at best, yet I didn't object. I let the judge handle it on my behalf, which only looked better in the eyes of the jury.

Unable to fluster Donna to the point of breaking down, Glynn moved on from her story of what happened to her personal medical history. While I realized this was a necessary evil, I felt it was hitting below the belt, so to speak. He had no tact when talking about her previous pregnancies, miscarriages, and fertility issues, and even her husband's sperm count.

The one blow Glynn did deliver was when he asked Donna if any doctor had told her, based on the chromosome testing she and Juan

had undergone, that they could *rule out* a genetic cause for John's condition. I objected to the question but was overruled, and Donna was
forced to answer.

"I have never asked a doctor that," she said.

While we knew Johnny's condition was not genetically based, this
single question and answer certainly left an indelible mark on the jury.
But how would Donna have known to ask such a question anyway?
It was up to my team to show the jury that Glynn and his team were
wrong.

Dead wrong.

# 15

AFTER DONNA'S TESTIMONY, I spent the next couple of days presenting testimony about how Benlate was used at the farm, especially on the two critical days in November 1989. My plan from the start was to methodically prove to the jury that, first, Donna Castillo was sprayed that fateful day, and, second, there *was* science to support the charge that Benlate caused Johnny's birth defect. I was prepared and determined to conclusively prove both points.

We spent two full days of the trial putting into evidence invoices that supported the purchase of Benlate; we put into evidence the amount of Benlate that could have been on hand on the day Donna was sprayed; we provided the testimony of Eddie Sanders, the driver of the tractor, as well as weather records showing the weather and wind conditions on those November days; and we had the testimony of plant experts who stated when Benlate would have been used—in this case, Benlate would have been used prophylactically in the early stages of growth after planting. In essence, we spent the entire two days proving the purchase and use of Benlate.

Once I had submitted all this evidence, it felt like a good time to play my ace card. The huge disconnect between the two defendants was painfully obvious, especially when I realized DuPont had no clue what was about to happen next. Neither did the codefendant, Pine Island Farms, who was the prey that got caught in my trap when they answered my sixty-five requests for admissions. As soon as I began to read Pine Island's responses aloud to the jury, both defendants realized my strategy and knew the damage this would do to their case.

"Your Honor, would you instruct the jury on the meaning of requests for admissions and related responses?"

The judge obliged. "Ladies and gentleman, a request for admission is a procedure whereby one party requests the other party to admit or deny certain statements of fact. An admission or denial by a party cannot be rebutted, opposed, or controverted in any way by the party that made such an admission or denial."

"Thank you, Your Honor. Ladies and gentleman, I am now going to read *sixty-four* requests for admissions that were served on Pine Island Farms prior to this trial." While I had served sixty-five requests, my plan was to read only sixty-four. I wasn't required to read them all.

This process took about thirty minutes, but what a game changer this half hour proved to be. I intentionally read each question and answer very slowly and deliberately so the jury could absorb each and every denial by Pine Island Farms.

"Ladies and gentleman, the *first* request for admission is as follows: admit or deny that Pine Island Farms was using the chemical **Trigard** at the U-Pick fields on or about November 1 or November 2, 1989. Answer: denied.

"Ladies and gentleman, the *second* request for admission is as follows: admit or deny that Pine Island Farms was using the chemical **Bravo** at the U-Pick fields on or about November 1 or November 2, 1989. Answer: denied."

I looked up at the jury every time, making eye contact with each member before proceeding with the next request for admission, all of which had been denied by Pine Island Farms. Somewhere around the ninth denial, I thought I heard pencils breaking in the courtroom as I continued to read. I briefly lifted my eyes from the papers in my hand to glance at the defendants' counsel table, where I saw both sides in a state of panic. They looked completely devastated by what was transpiring.

It had become excruciatingly clear to them that these denials would have a catastrophic impact on their case. Pine Island Farms was bound by their own denials that any of these products could have possibly come from the tractor Donna described. That left only Benlate.

When I read that last admission—the sixty-fourth out of the sixty-five I had submitted—I felt as though I had won a major victory on the exposure battle. There was no doubt in my mind that if the members of the jury believed Donna Castillo had been sprayed that day, there could be no other explanation as to what the substance in the spray was except Benlate. One by one, I had knocked out every other possibility.

While no one from the defendants' side could object, you can bet they quickly asked Judge Donner for a sidebar. "Judge, that's not fair. Mr. Ferraro served sixty-five requests for admissions to the farm, and he read only sixty-four," Gaebe pleaded with the judge, sounding more like a sniveling schoolboy than seasoned trial lawyer.

"Judge, we just spent the last two days putting multiple witnesses on the stand and placing into evidence all sorts of information about Benlate. I am under no legal obligation to read their denial—or their admission, for that matter—as evidence in my case," I stated very emphatically.

"But that's not fair!" Gaebe whined.

"Counsel, whether you think it's fair or not isn't the issue. Mr. Ferraro is correct. He doesn't need to read that sixty-fifth response.

Unfortunately, counsel, that's the law," Judge Donner said as she dismissed us back to our respective corners of the courtroom. In Gaebe's haste to defend his client, he had freely and carelessly used the word "denied" and ended up accidentally speaking the truth.

"Counsel, if you're ready, let's move on to your next witness," the judge said to me.

# 16

WITH THE EXPOSURE issue now firmly behind us, the next fight we had to endure was the battle of science.

Since the very start of the trial, DuPont had been disseminating all sorts of propaganda about their product and the case itself. They primarily used press releases to send a message that this case was a bunch of crap. They even went so far as to say their own rat studies weren't indicative of anything relevant.

In addition to the press releases, they had witnesses testify that a person would have to drink at least five gallons of the chemical benomyl, to replicate the amount the rats were given in the studies, to cause any real damage to a human embryo or fetus. This was downright absurd, if not insulting, to Johnny and to every other victim. The defense went so far as to say that anything in excess—including drinking too much water—could potentially kill people—which it can, but you have to drink enormous amounts for it to be dangerous. Yeah, that's how down and dirty they got, which wasn't all that unusual in high-stakes cases such as this one, but these kinds of tactics certainly didn't make our position any easier.

This overt attempt to discredit the rat studies by continually calling them junk science throughout discovery and now during the trial kept me up many nights. Why were the studies *great* science when they needed them to get approved by the EPA, but now they were *junk* science when we wanted to use the results against them? Tactically, I understood the attempt they were making, but they didn't have an ethical leg to stand on.

No company would put so much effort or money into such studies if they meant nothing to them. They certainly weren't testing Benlate or benomyl at certain specific dose levels to prove nothing. The big question plaguing my thoughts at this point was, Where in the world was this five-gallon analogy coming from, and how does it possibly make any sense? In my mind, it was absolutely absurd, and I needed to prove that to the jury. That was critical.

I started doing the math. First I converted gallons to milligrams. Since all the scientific measurements had been taken using the metric system, I thought it would be tougher for the jury to follow along without this initial conversion. Because it was going to be difficult enough for them to understand the complexity of the math at hand, I had to make it as easy to comprehend as possible. Next, I took the weights of the rats that were used in the study and compared them to the amounts of benomyl they were given to find a weight-to-dosage ratio. Then I plugged in Donna Castillo's weight at the time she was sprayed to get the comparable amount of the chemical for a person of her size. As it turned out, the amount of benomyl needed wasn't five gallons at all, but merely one-fortieth of an ounce!

Because I hadn't gotten Dr. Brent to generally admit in his deposition that the 1982 Staples numbers were a lie, I knew I had to get one of the defense's other experts, Dr. Judith C. Stadler, to admit it under oath in front of the jury. But working with numbers and science is not as easy as it sounds, especially when you're dealing with a seasoned scientist like Dr. Stadler.

When DuPont realized I had found and then broken down the Staples studies, I believe the company thought it could overcome the obvious discrepancies in its research by bringing in Dr. Stadler as a witness. She was a senior research toxicologist and head of the inhalation toxicology group at the DuPont laboratory. In its answers to interrogatories, DuPont listed her as one of the top three most knowledgeable people in the world about the chemical benomyl and the product Benlate, even going so far as to make her the corporate representative for the trial. DuPont wanted to humanize itself by presenting a face at the trial to address these issues, and admittedly, Dr. Stadler was a good strategic choice. She looked the part, dressing and acting like a conservative professor or a stately, middle-aged high-school teacher.

The interesting thing about having corporate reps attend a trial is that sometimes they're called to testify and sometimes they aren't. In this case, I expected Glynn would put Dr. Stadler on the stand to say what a great company DuPont was and how responsible and safe their scientists were in conducting their research. Instead of waiting for Glynn, however, I thought the better move would be for *me* to call Dr. Stadler in my case as an *adverse* witness. Dr. Stadler was clearly adverse, as she was DuPont's corporate representative at the trial. Normally, leading questions are allowed only in cross-examination of witnesses; the exception is with adverse witnesses, who can legitimately be asked leading questions in direct examination. I felt it was critical that I be able to ask Dr. Stadler leading questions because it was crucial for me to have the ability to simplify complicated concepts for the jury. My strategy was to break down the math into easy steps so I could get Dr. Stadler to admit that my analysis was correct. Math can be such a powerful tool when used correctly, because numbers don't lie.

My primary objective with Dr. Stadler was to completely dismantle the bullshit five-gallon theory that had been touted by DuPont.

Dr. Stadler presented very well and appeared quite poised as she sat in the courtroom each day awaiting her turn on the stand. I purposely joked with her every now and then by saying, "Today may be your day, Judy." I did my best to be kind and charming. I wanted to keep her both on edge and off guard for when she was actually called to the witness stand.

And then, on May 29, I finally called her.

Once Dr. Stadler was sworn in, I quickly got her to testify that she had spent more than two hundred hours preparing for the trial by reviewing the Staples studies (both Staples I and Staples II), the Hoogenboom study, and a whole variety of other relevant studies, and that she had analyzed them, made comparisons, and reached certain determinations. But even with that level of preparation, she appeared a little unsure of herself at first.

I then questioned Dr. Stadler at length about how the compound enters the bloodstream of rats. She explained that when you gavage a rat (directly introduce a chemical, drug, or food item through a tube into the stomach during a clinical trial), you're going to get a lot of absorption into the bloodstream, which directly relates to the effects the study reveals.

"When doing a gavage study, the compound is placed right into a rat's stomach or digestive tract, right?" I asked.

Dr. Stadler said yes, explaining that when it comes to humans, there are some things that pass right through the bloodstream unabsorbed and others that are absorbed, such as medications.

Next, since the studies were done using the metric system, I came up with ten simple calculations that converted the metric units to units the jury could understand. My goal was to calculate the amount of benomyl it would take for enough to pass through the skin, enter the bloodstream, and impact a human embryo or fetus.

I put together a ten-step chart so the jury and Dr. Stadler could easily follow my simple math conversions. As soon as I began my line of questioning, Clem Glynn objected. To my surprise, he suddenly proclaimed to the court that "Dr. Stadler isn't an expert." According to him, she had not been designated as an expert, and the fact that she was a corporate representative did not open the door to start eliciting expert opinions from her, let alone asking her to perform mathematical calculations.

Of course, my position was very different. I thought she was quite qualified, because she was listed as one of the three most knowledgeable people on earth about Benlate and had testified earlier that she had a substantial background in math. All I was asking her to do was take some simple metric system numbers, apply them to the gavage doses used in the Staples studies to obtain a ratio, and then help apply that ratio to a one hundred seventy pound adult like Donna Castillo to see just how small the "big" dose DuPont said was required really was. I thought Dr. Stadler was more than capable and qualified to do that.

The judge agreed with me. She pointed out that, by definition, an expert witness is not a specialist—it's a person whose testimony helps decide an ultimate issue for the jury. An expert is somebody who, by special skill, training, or experience, is allowed to testify in the form of opinions.

Dr. Stadler had been designated a corporate representative by DuPont. Either she was just a body to make it look like corporations are people, or she was a person with knowledge. In this case, she was a toxicologist, which meant I could ask her any questions of fact related to the case that only an expert witness could answer for the jury. I was totally within my bounds, especially since DuPont had identified her as the person within the company who, because of her vast knowledge, could address questions about the studies.

My tactics may have flustered Dr. Stadler, but they really got to opposing counsel. Throughout the trial, every time they suspected I might begin to circle a witness like a hungry shark, Glynn, Gaebe, or one of the other attorneys from their teams objected, whether there was a legitimate basis for an objection or not. This was their way of interrupting the testimony and confusing the jury. To be fair, I may have and probably did do the same thing. The constant objecting from the attorneys on both sides eventually irritated the judge, which usually resulted in a flurry of sidebar conversations between her and counsel at her bench.

During sidebars, the jury is not supposed to hear any of the dialogue between the lawyers and the judge. Anything the jury hears can affect credibility and plant seeds of doubt. Initially, however, the DuPont team, led by Glynn, would jockey for position at Judge Donner's bench and speak loudly enough for the jury to hear. Glynn would then proceed to make self-serving statements, such as "Your Honor, that's a fraud," while facing in the direction of the jury. Since you can't directly address the jury at any time during the trial except during jury selection, opening statements, and closing arguments, DuPont thought these loud and improper sidebars might help their cause. This immature and completely manipulative behavior really got me angry. It had to stop. Initially trying to play the part of the good guy, I pleaded with Glynn, asking him to keep it down. "The jury can hear you," I'd say, but to no avail. When it didn't stop, I realized that if I wanted to be in the game, I had to meet my enemy eye to eye, and so decided I would race to the pole position and do the same thing to him. Glynn was twelve years older than me and had a bit of a problem with his hip at the time, so he wasn't nearly as fast getting to the bench as I was. He also had to cover a slightly greater distance from his table than I had to from mine, so I could beat him to the mark almost every time. After finally realizing that his nonsense had backfired on him, Glynn began pleading with me to stop doing it to them. The antics eventually ended.

It appeared that everything we were doing, even something as mundane as meeting at the bench, was a duel to the bitter end. Strategy and gamesmanship in the courtroom—even stupid stuff like this—can sometimes make or break a case. It isn't unusual for legal teams to hire investigators to hang around within earshot of the jury and strike up a conversation centering around the trial, saying such things as "This case is bullshit" or "The family should really be ashamed of themselves for bringing a case like this." While lawyers can't talk to the jurors, some will try to get other people to talk around them. It's awful, disgraceful, and, frankly, the worst part of going up against a conglomerate like DuPont. While not all lawyers are ruthless and without moral judgment, many will practice such guerrilla warfare when it comes to a case like this.

Once the judge cleared my line of questioning, I began slowly and meticulously walking Dr. Stadler through each of my ten mathematical calculations, some as simple as clarifying how many ounces there are in a pound. "Doctor, these calculations will all relate to a simulated gavage exposure based on the Staples study. Would you agree that the 1982 Staples study came up with a low effect level of 62.5 milligrams per kilogram per day of exposure to benomyl?"

"That's right."

"Would you also agree the 1980 Staples study came up with a low effect level of 10 milligrams per kilogram per day of exposure to benomyl?"

"That's right, but it's disputed."

"And the milligrams are the amount of the chemical, and the kilogram measurement is the amount of the body weight, right?"

"That's right."

"Would you convert kilos to kilograms (1000 grams per kilo) and compare milligrams (1000 milligrams per gram) to kilograms? Doctor, if you need my chart or a calculator at any point, please let me know, because I am aware this is confusing, because a kilogram is one thousand grams, and a milligram is one-thousandth of a gram. So basically, in Staples 1982, we are talking about 62.5 millionths of a kilo? Does that sound correct? I still have a calculator if you need to calculate it."

When I asked whether Dr. Stadler wanted to use my calculator and then held it out for her to see if it would make things easier, the jury chuckled, which was unintentional on my part. After all, wasn't she one of the three top experts in the world?

Dr. Stadler didn't like my methodology, but she didn't disagree with my math.

"Would you agree that an ounce is 28.35 grams?" As she tried to anticipate where I was going with this, she began to appear uncomfortable and was unable to answer even the simplest questions.

"I'm not sure about that. I don't have anything right now to say that's true," she said.

"Do you know anyone in the toxicology department at DuPont who knows how many grams are in an ounce?"

"There are probably people who know it. Offhand, I always look it up if I try to do a conversion."

"Does 28.35 grams sound familiar to you?"

"I honestly do not know."

"Let's operate under the assumption that's correct. What I'm doing is converting this .625 to grams so we can start to make our conversion to ounces, because we want to get to a bottom line that is in ounces. In other words, what we're doing here is taking .000625 kilograms and making it into grams. To do that, we're knocking off three decimal places."

"I'm sorry. I'm not used to doing this."

"Doctor, just take your time. Again, I have a calculator if you need it," I said. Clearly, Dr. Stadler was getting flustered. "And to make kilograms into grams, you would simply make one thousand grams, correct?" I said, knowing there was nothing simple about this.

"That's right," she agreed.

At this point, the judge could also see that Dr. Stadler was uneasy and offered to have the bailiff bring her a calculator that converted ounces to grams and so on. While she wouldn't take the calculator from me, she gladly accepted it from the bailiff. Once she did, she was able to follow along with the rest of my calculations, including the assumption that at the time of her exposure, Donna Castillo weighed 170 pounds.

"I assume you know how many ounces are in a pound?"

"Sixteen."

"Correct. So that would make 170 pounds how many ounces?"

"I don't think she weighed that much."

"She doesn't today, but unfortunately, during her pregnancy, I think that's what she weighed."

"Objection to counsel's comment as to fortunate or unfortunate," Glynn said.

"Sustained."

"If Mrs. Castillo weighed 170 pounds, which equals 2,720 ounces, she would weigh 77.11 kilograms, right?"

"That sounds about right."

"You recall that there are 28.35 grams in an ounce, correct?"

"Yes."

"According to my calculations doctor, 2720 oz. x 28.35 g. = 77,112 g. Then you divide that by 1000 to get 77.11 kg. Now, you come up with the total ounces of active ingredient for her body weight, which equals 0.1619, approximately one-sixth of an ounce over the course of an entire day of exposure, if you converted the Staples 1982 study number of 62.5 to an adult the size of Mrs. Castillo, correct?"

"One-sixth of an ounce taken by gavage, that is correct."

"Then if you went to the 1980 Staples study and you accepted his methodology and the written statement in his summary that the low level effect level was ten milligrams per kilogram per day, you would simply divide the 62.5 by 10, and now the number becomes one-fortieth of an ounce by gavage exposure for Mrs. Castillo."

Although Dr. Stadler fought against answering each calculation, especially the last one, and Glynn objected to my mischaracterization of the study, the judge overruled the objection and Dr. Stadler was forced to answer, essentially agreeing with each of my calculations. Once I got her to admit to each number on the list of ten, she was left extremely flustered and confused.

At that point, I went back through each step of the calculations that she had just verified as mathematically correct, following them one by one to the conclusion that it would take only one-fortieth of an ounce of Benlate to seep into the skin and then the bloodstream to impact the fetus of Donna Castillo—not five gallons, as had been suggested over and over. I absolutely needed to make this point clear to the jury through one of the defendants' own witnesses.

Once Dr. Stadler had said yes to the math, she had no option but to say yes to the premise I was attempting to prove, even if she said it kicking and screaming. I continued my questioning for several more hours, refusing to let up on Dr. Stadler. I asked her to comment on the possibility of a bystander being exposed to Benlate mist as opposed to a user of the product, such as a farm worker.

"Your Honor, I object on the grounds it is improper use of testimony," Glynn jumped in.

"Overruled."

Dr. Stadler replied, "I would say that certainly that would not be what you would expect if the material is being used according to the label, but it would certainly be possible. If there was some kind of drift, then a bystander could possibly be exposed."

"Doctor, are you aware of recent statements made by DuPont in which the corporation has stated or put out information that one would have to drink two pints of Benlate mix to get the conditions microphthalmia and anophthalmia in humans?"

"I object to the form of the question," Glynn said. "It mischaracterizes the evidence."

"Overruled."

Dr. Stadler answered, "I am aware of a number of estimates of how much you might have to drink that would be similar to a gavage dose. I'm not specifically aware of two pints being one of the numbers. I think a number of different people have made estimates. I've heard many different statements by many different people."

This was such a typical non-answer by the defense's own corporate representative.

After a long and grueling testimony, it boiled down to one last question: "Doctor, after benomyl gets through the skin of a human, where does it go?"

"Where does it go?" she repeated.

"Yes, through the skin of a human; where would it go?" I asked once more.

"It's going to slowly—very slowly—get into the bloodstream," she softly replied.

Bingo. I had her.

"No further questions," I said and turned to the jury, smiled, and walked back to my desk. I was slowly dismantling DuPont's proverbial house, and after Dr. Stadler's testimony, I believed they knew it.

I think the whole "five-gallon" propaganda tactic by DuPont and their lawyers was a foolish approach. It hurt their case. I think the better practice for defense attorneys is to be surgical in their approach. They should be willing to focus on only one or two solid issues they completely believe are right. Those who take a more surgical approach to the facts are far more persuasive than defense attorneys who say everything about the case is wrong. The real surgeons admit many facts yet pounce on the few flaws they're certain are fatal. To be challenged by such an opponent is rare. It definitely ups your game as a plaintiff attorney. There's no doubt that those lawyers are harder to beat.

On the plaintiff side, we often have to prove a lot in order to win. If we miss one point, we lose. It's like building a house: if you take a single brick out of the foundation, the whole house becomes unstable and falls. Game over. That isn't how it works on the defense side, where in some cases it takes only knocking a single brick out of place to win. Glynn was definitely good enough to do that, but he didn't.

DuPont goes to great lengths to indoctrinate its lawyers into thinking its way. It pays them top dollar and will do things such as wire attorneys' fees to their accounts immediately upon receipt of bills without question (no matter how outrageous the bills may be) in order to get them to drink the Kool-Aid. And from my perspective, Glynn certainly drank the Kool-Aid. It was clear to me that Glynn was so in love with this company that he would do anything for them.

One morning I said to Glynn, "Why are you so enamored with your dirtbag client, DuPont?"

Instead of defending the dirtbag comment, he explained to me that this was his best client. He told me that when he sends a bill, they never question it, and within twenty-four hours, every penny is in his bank account.

Hearing this made sense to me. When you have a company that does bad things as a client, it can't directly offer its lawyers bribes or anything of an illegal nature, but it can surely do things within the legal limits like paying bills quickly and without question. It's a tacit sort of love affair.

Judge Donner released the jury for the day, as the stormy south Florida weather had become a concern for everyone in the courtroom. It was raining hard, and the judge wanted the jurors to get home safely. The courtroom was adjourned until 9:00 a.m. the following morning.

# 17

I spent the next week or so calling every expert witness in our arsenal to testify about the scientific evidence we had gathered to prove that once Donna had been exposed to the Benlate spray, the effect was clear: her son was born with no eyes.

These testimonies were tedious, complicated, and very tough on the jury. They had to endure hours of scientific explanations from our army of thirteen different authorities, each of whom helped establish our case one piece at a time. We had enlisted a biologist, a chemist, an ocularist, and a neuro-ophthalmologist, as well as multiple developmental toxicologists, spray drift analysts, teratologists, and, of course, a fetal pathologist—someone who could speak to the jury about what happened to Johnny while he was in the womb.

One of our key witnesses, Dr. Vyvyan Howard, had no prior experience testifying in our legal system, which made taking him into an American courtroom as an expert witness a great challenge. In fact, Dr. Howard had little experience testifying anywhere at all. He was colorful but not flamboyant. The wire-rimmed glasses he wore on the end of his nose made him look like a long-lost relative of George Washington or a character I'd once seen in an old painting hanging in the bathroom of a British castle. He looked, acted, and was the epitome of a highly educated man. When he walked into a room, you felt his intellect. You knew from the instant he opened his mouth that he spoke from a genuine wealth of knowledge. Without a doubt, I knew he could be a good witness. I believed he was honest, and I knew the jury would believe that, too. He was passionate about everything he said. He absolutely wanted to live in a better, safer world and had a deep desire to see that people weren't unnecessarily exposed to unsafe toxins.

Dr. Howard's educational background was indeed impressive. He was a medically qualified doctor from the United Kingdom. He held bachelor's degrees in medicine and surgery, which are the equivalents of MDs in the United States. He also earned a PhD in philosophy, the thesis for which required him to study the development of the brain. Furthermore, he was a member of the Royal College of Pathologists and of the British Society of Toxicological Pathologists. Dr. Howard had taught at the University of Liverpool School of Medicine since 1972; had been the general editor of the *Journal of Microscopy*, which is the journal of the Royal Microscopical Society, for seven years; and had been on the board of a number of other journals including *Acta Stereologica*. He had published at least sixty-seven papers on a number of topics centered around his studies and had an international reputation as a lecturer in the fields of quantitative microscopy and developmental toxicopathology. Regardless of his inexperience testifying in court, I really believed that with those kinds of credentials, the jury would see Dr. Howard as a serious and extremely qualified witness.

However, as mentioned before, the one big, overriding concern I had about Dr. Howard was his incessant use of the word "possible." Now was the moment of truth. Would Dr. Howard be able to withstand cross-examination and maintain his newfound scientific vocabulary conversion, or would he fold under the pressure? It was essential that Dr. Howard convert science's language of *possibilities* (anything less than 95 percent) into the court's language of *probabilities* (anything greater than 50 percent). Essentially, Dr. Howard had to maintain his reprogramming in order to tell the truth in the court's language. Now was the time to see whether all my efforts to break him of his annoying habit had paid off. One thing was for sure: when he arrived to testify, he understood I was as serious as a heart attack when it came to this particular matter.

I called Dr. Howard to the stand on May 22, three weeks into the trial. By this point, the jury had heard a lot of evidence that I hoped had already convinced them to hold DuPont and Pine Island Farms responsible for Johnny Castillo's birth defect as a result of Donna's exposure to Benlate. My goal with Dr. Howard was to seal the deal. After the testimony of my other expert witnesses before him, I needed Dr. Howard to leave no room for doubt in the jurors' minds.

DuPont's contention from the very start of the trial was that Dr. Howard was not qualified to be an expert witness. But then again, the company made that same claim about Dr. Stadler—its own corporate representative. I slowly introduced Dr. Howard to the court and the jury by going through his impressive résumé with them. Glynn objected. Apparently, the résumé I was using was an updated version of the one that had been submitted into evidence when I had added Dr. Howard to my list of witnesses several months earlier. Judge Donner reviewed the new résumé, which was twelve pages longer. The reality is, the court can't stop a witness from updating his or her résumé—but to be fair, the judge wanted clarity regarding the differences between the two documents. The new version noted additional research grants and lecture appearances. It also included some narrative that had not been on Dr. Howard's previous résumé, which made the new one more impressive. At the court's request, I had to ask the witness to state for the record how the two résumé's were different before I could continue.

Dr. Howard explained that at his last deposition, he had been asked to produce a more current résumé, which, given his busy schedule, was difficult to keep updated, so he had added to it sporadically since then. The new résumé was simply more detailed and current. This formality took well over an hour and proved to be completely fruitless for the defendants. If anything, it showed that Dr. Howard was even more qualified to be sitting in that courtroom.

Once we were able to get back to the matter at hand, I began to take Dr. Howard into the subject of teratology. This, of course, was where Glynn felt Dr. Howard had no proper training.

"Dr. Howard, what does 'teratology' mean?" I asked.

"Well, strictly, it comes from the Greek word meaning the study of monstrosities or monsters."

"And how does that relate to the practice of medicine today?"

"Well, different groups of medical practitioners and, indeed, scientists are interested in malformations, and they can all practice teratology. So geneticists, developmental pathologists, scientists working in toxicology with animals can all study teratology, which is really showing an interest in developing creatures or fetuses."

"Does it study birth defects?"

"Yes."

"Doctor, is that what you spend some of your time doing as a developmental toxicologist and pathologist?"

"Yes, I spend a considerable amount of my time doing that. About ninety percent of my time."

"Doctor, have you been asked to consider the evidence in this case and form an opinion as to the cause of microphthalmia in the plaintiff, John Castillo?"

"Yes, I have. It is my opinion that, within a reasonable degree of medical and scientific probability, the case of microphthalmia in John Castillo was caused by his mother's exposure to benomyl during a critical stage in the development of his eyes."

Dr. Howard went on to describe how in rat studies benomyl was found to interfere with the cellular division process by stopping the formation of tubulin, one of the basic proteins in the cells of animals. Tubulin is needed to form microtubules. These microtubules are required for a number of processes in the cell. When the cell starts to divide, it builds a skeleton along which chromosomes can migrate during division. That skeleton is made of tubulin. Tubulin is also involved in what's called cell motility—the ability of a cell to move or for movement to occur within cells. All these capabilities, including cell proliferation, cells being able to move around, and cells being able to grow, are required for the normal development of the nervous system. Interestingly, the process described by Dr. Howard works exactly the same in plants, animals, and humans.

In this particular case, Dr. Howard saw a lot of evidence—in fact, he reviewed over four thousand pages of documentation in his laboratory, which enabled him to assess the different possible ways exposure occurs. Ingestion (eating), inhalation (breathing), or transdermal or dermal assimilation (through the skin) were the only viable methods in this case. In addition to Dr. Howard, we had the twelve other experts, including a geneticist, a chemist, a neuro-ophthalmologist, a developmental toxicologist, an OB/GYN, a fetal pathologist, and more. But Dr. Howard was the most important expert because he was, in essence, the captain of the team. He did what is known as a "differential diagnosis." A differential diagnosis is the process by which other possible causes, if any, are ruled out. It's commonly done throughout medicine and, for that matter, in many other scientific disciplines. Simply put, it is a process of elimination. Here, Dr. Howard's differential diagnosis covered both the mode of exposure (ingestion, inhalation, or dermal) and the process of ruling out specific environmental causes (e.g., vitamin K, hypothermia, etc.).

How did he do this?

First, Dr. Howard looked at ingestion. We all have minute traces of various chemicals in our bodies, which get in through our diets. Benomyl is one of those chemicals that can possibly be taken in by eating, but since anything that goes through the stomach also goes through the liver, where it's detoxified and then excreted by the kidneys, diet was an unlikely consideration in this case, although it could be one port of entry.

Next Dr. Howard considered inhalation as a means of exposure. At the time, DuPont had released the results of a study it conducted that suggested benomyl could be inhaled from a spray. Dr. Howard made some calculations based on the results of that study as well as those of another study performed in England at DuPont ICI (Imperial Chemical Industries), which sells benomyl or Benlate under license from DuPont. Those calculations convinced Dr. Howard that inhalation was not a likely cause of Donna Castillo's exposure.

Finally, Dr. Howard explored dermal transmission through the skin. As it happened, DuPont ICI also did a study that looked at transmission rates through human skin. The ICI study took human skin from fresh female postmortem specimens; put it into a special petri dish, which the researchers painted with a standard solution of benomyl at a known concentration; and then measured how much benomyl transported itself through the skin over the course of twenty-four hours. This study provided a quantitative measure of the amount of Benlate that could actually be transported into the body if the skin was contaminated. Transdermal absorption was a major consideration in this case. Dr. Howard assessed this as the most likely form of exposure that caused Johnny to be born with no eyes.

One of the significant features in the case was the fact that there had been quite a strong wind blowing on the day Donna Castillo was exposed. We had shown this to be true through her testimony, but we also substantiated it with weather charts, records of prevailing meteorological conditions at the time, and expert-witness testimony. When it comes to a substance like Benlate, air is a transport mechanism.

Air will carry droplets of liquid and deposit them on the skin. This can happen on uncovered skin as well on the skin of a person who is lightly clothed, provided they are doused with enough of the liquid. The source of the droplets on this day was a tank attached to the sprayer, which contained a mixture of water and Benlate. As this liquid was sprayed from the tank, each droplet maintained the same concentration of Benlate as it had in the tank. When the chemical gets deposited on the skin of a person, such as Donna Castillo, it is called "dermal exposure." If water evaporates from the droplet at any point, the concentration of Benlate within the droplet will rise, because Benlate is a nonvolatile substance. Unfortunately, Benlate does not evaporate like water.

According to Dr. Howard, and based on the information we had from the DuPont ICI studies, once Benlate is deposited on a subject's skin, it will start to be assimilated through dermal transfer at a measured rate of 3 percent. This means that while the majority of the Benlate deposited on Donna's skin remained on the surface during the length of her exposure (from the time the drops landed on her until she showered), 3 percent of the total portion made its way through the epidermis, was picked up by the capillaries under the skin, and then was transported through the veins and into the heart. From the heart, it was sent to the lungs where the blood was oxygenated, returned down to the left side of the heart, and was ultimately pumped out into the circulation system, which extends to everything in the body. This is called the "systemic side" of the circulation system. The blood, which will now have benomyl in it if the chemical has been absorbed through the skin, will reach the placenta. Once there, molecules of benomyl's size, which are really quite small, have no difficulty traveling across the placenta and reaching the developing fetus.

To better understand this process, it's critical to note that it doesn't take much of the chemical to make an impact. Molecules are measured in terms of molecular weight. Substances with a molecular weight of less than 1,000 grams per mol have little trouble getting through the placenta. Certainly those with a molecular weight of less than 400 g/mol can be absorbed even more quickly. Most drugs—and, indeed, benomyl—fall into this category. In rat studies, benomyl was able to get to the embryo or fetus very easily, so the assumption is that it would be able to get through in humans, too. Remember that 80 percent of the time something happens in rats, it also happens in humans.

Next, Dr. Howard began to talk about the many different ways an embryo or fetus can be impacted by environmental factors, including Benlate. He went on to methodically rule out any other known potential environmental cause that could have affected Donna Castillo. He considered and ruled out vitamin K; he considered and ruled out excessive time spent in hot tubs; he considered and ruled out anything else that could possibly have been involved in this incident.

When he had finished with that part of his testimony, he then spoke at length about the process of arrested development and complete cell death (which, by the way, occurs when more than 75 percent of the cell is affected). In his opinion, that was what happened to Johnny's eyes.

In one of the studies conducted by Dr. Dick Van Velzen—done at Dr. Howard's request—cells were cultured in various concentrations of benomyl and then measured for something known as neurite retraction. In a solution of only three parts per billion of Benlate, the researchers measured a significant reduction in the outgrowth of neurites. If such a process were occurring during Johnny's gestation and the eye cells were waiting for alarm bells to go off, they would not have had the right functional connections to alert them, and the cells would likely have perished as a result. In Dr. Howard's opinion, this is what caused Johnny's birth defect.

In this test, the cells would either divide normally or something would go wrong because the scaffold on which the chromosomes usually migrated hadn't formed properly. If something goes wrong in a fetal cell, it just rolls up and dies. Scientists can actually measure the rate at which this happens with a micronucleus test. If you have cells that are dying, it's because they have been exposed to something harmful. During the developmental process, cells pass through what is called a window of vulnerability. When the eyes, for instance, are in their most critical stage of development, or maximal proliferation, that's the time when they are most susceptible to certain sorts of injury. This specific window of vulnerability is also known as organogenesis. Organogenesis in humans occurs from week three of gestation to week eight. During that time a number of different structures will form at different intervals. The window of vulnerability for the eyes is during this stage. If the optic vessel is forming and something happens to affect the process, no eye will develop at all; anophthalmia is the result. That wasn't exactly the case with Johnny. His cells sustained injury slightly later in organogenesis, so he developed some ocular tissue, which presented as tiny cysts in the orbits where the globes (eyes) would normally be. In other words, the later in the process the arrested development occurs, the greater the chance that there will be some eye formation, even if it's very, very minimal.

The first phase of Dr. Howard's testimony took a full day. It was clear and concise, and made extremely difficult scientific information easy to understand. I suggested that we adjourn for the day at the end of the first phase, as I knew the next portion of my questioning would be more complicated and I wanted the jury to be fresh when they heard the rest of what Dr. Howard had to say. It had been a long day for everyone. The judge agreed, releasing Dr. Howard from the witness stand and sending the jury home until the following morning.

We had done a good job, but there was still a lot of work ahead of us.

As we had almost every night of the trial, Liz Russo and I went back to my office to recap the day and go over our notes. Ana Rivero typically brought very little to the table. Liz and I were the ones who bounced substantive ideas back and forth. We'd have deep and sometimes heated conversations while Ana sat there like a fly on the wall.

Every night she'd say something that was totally confounding, to the point where I'd have to bite my tongue to avoid going absolutely bat-shit crazy on her. Admittedly, this case was extremely complicated and challenging, and she was relatively new to it, but by the time I realized she was in way over her head it was too late to take her off the team. I wanted to give her the benefit of the doubt that she'd have a bright future, but for the purposes of this case, I had to write her off. I would do my best to ignore her and just move on with strategizing our next moves for the following day in court with Liz, though there were plenty of times I had to tell Ana to go home before I lost my cool. DuPont and Pine Island Farms made sure the evidence was always a moving target. We'd have to think through all the possible angles in advance so we'd be prepared for anything they would try to throw at us. That meant lots of talking things through. The last thing I wanted or needed at the end of a long and tedious day in court was an annoying associate who added no value to the game. The only person I could have any meaningful conversations with about this case was Liz.

The following morning, Dr. Howard took the stand once again. The dialogue that ensued focused on the rate at which benomyl penetrated the skin. Employing a micropipette—a scientifically calibrated instrument frequently used in labs to measure out specific amounts of liquid—Dr. Howard showed the jury the small amount of benomyl (20 microliters) that was used in the ICI study. Drawing from the pipette, he proceeded to drop the 20 microliters into my hand. It was instantly clear that a droplet that small wouldn't even cover the fingernail on Donna's pinky. Dr. Howard then went on to explain at length the chemistry of the breaking down of chemicals—specifically benomyl—in the liver. The body takes benomyl and converts it into hydroxy 5MBC and carbendazim. All three are toxic to the body, and the effects they have on the developing eye are the same.

Eventually the body wants to get rid of this stuff, which means it has to make it more water-soluble to get it through the kidneys and to release it. It's quite a fast process, and we have lots of microsomes in our cells that help make it happen. Unfortunately, the embryo or fetus cannot do this on its own, so it relies on the mother to take the hydroxy 5MBC out.

Next, Dr. Howard laid out his chemical exposure calculation, which was based on the amount of the surface area of Donna Castillo's skin that was exposed to the chemical on the day she was doused. Donna's total body surface area came to 18,800 square centimeters. Because she was wearing shorts and a sleeveless top that day, leaving her face, neck, arms, and legs uncovered, Dr. Howard estimated that half of that total surface—9,400 square centimeters of skin—was exposed directly to benomyl that day. That was equal to 9,400 times the fingernail-sized amount we had demonstrated moments earlier in the courtroom.

At the given dermal transmission rate, 49 micrograms of benomyl per square centimeter was transmitted through Donna's skin during each hour that passed until she showered. If you multiply that by the total number of square centimeters of Donna's skin that was exposed, it would create an amount of benomyl in her bloodstream in the hundreds of parts per billion.

With exposure to doses this high, we knew benomyl was the cause. We just had to prove it. Dr. Howard then systematically went through each of the studies to back up his findings, including DuPont's, ICI's, and Dr. Van Velzen's in vitro tests, which showed cell death, otherwise known or "apoptosis," occurring at amounts as low as 22 parts per billion (PPB). Even worse, we had the evidence of neurite retraction at 3 PPB.

By the end of day two, I thought we had made a very strong case. Dr. Howard had done an excellent job stating the facts and had been a terrific witness on direct exam for the Castillos. But we weren't completely out of the woods yet, as Glynn still had to cross-examine him.

Glynn came out with both guns loaded. His first order of business was to try to get Dr. Howard stricken as a witness. He argued that the doctor's entire testimony should be tossed out because it was based on assumptions that there was no possibility of a genetic cause for Johnny Castillo's birth defect. While that had not been an issue when Dr. Howard's deposition was taken, a defense witness later stated under oath that an underlying genetic factor was a "possibility." Despite that testimony, Dr. Howard still believed the cause of Johnny's microphthalmia was environmental (that is, benomyl) and not genetic. He stood firmly behind his testimony, his calculations, and the lack of scientific evidence indicating a genetic cause. The judge agreed and wouldn't allow Glynn to strike Dr. Howard. There simply was no evidence of a genetic link to Johnny's microphthalmia. DuPont took the position that science had not yet developed to the point where a genetic cause could be established. In other words, DuPont's position was that we should be forced to prove a negative.

Part of DuPont's defense was that the cause of microphthalmia was either genetics or environment, but never both. Dr. Howard's position, which today is generally accepted science, was that most birth defects are a combination of genetics and environment, or "genetic susceptibility." Some people are simply more genetically susceptible to environmental factors. This opinion not only made scientific sense, it also made common sense.

Unable to win that battle with his first strategy, Glynn had to dismantle Dr. Howard's testimony piece by piece in front of the jury. It was apparent that he would stop at nothing in his attempt to do so. The first fault he found in Dr. Howard's testimony was his insistence that inhalation was not a real factor. When Glynn questioned Dr. Howard about why he thought it might have been a possibility during his deposition but no longer seemed to think it was during his court testimony, Dr. Howard explained that the testimony of spray expert William Hunt gave him pause. Hunt had testified about the wind conditions on the day Donna Castillo was exposed. That testimony changed Dr. Howard's opinion post-deposition.

While that might have satisfied a less savvy or experienced attorney, Glynn was just getting started. He confronted Dr. Howard with an error he had made on some of the work he did for this case. He specifically cited an overestimation based on a DuPont document known as the Waritz Memorandum. This document was not a scientific study but rather a calculation estimating two things: how far a spray could carry benomyl to a person who would then inhale it, and, once that happened, how much benomyl would make it into the body's tissues. In the transposition from imperial units to metric units, Dr. Howard had made an error by a factor of ten, which increased the amount of spray mix Donna Castillo would have been able to inhale tenfold.

Glynn then introduced a document written in March 1996 into evidence, wherein Dr. Howard offered his opinion regarding the possibility that inhalation was the primary cause of Johnny's microphthalmia. It read, "As has been described in detail before, the principle component of Mrs. Castillo's acute benomyl exposure was inhalational and could in my opinion have led to plasma levels in the range." Dr. Howard did his best to explain that there was some discussion about the effect of wind speed and he was going to work on some new calculations, but this document certainly contradicted two days of testimony.

As Liz and I sat and listened to Dr. Howard, I noticed her scribbling on her legal pad. She often doodled when she got nervous. Liz leaned over and showed me a drawing that appeared to be Dr. Howard on the witness stand, slowly slumping in his chair as Glynn continued with his beat down. I didn't want to smile at the image she had created, since Dr. Howard was our expert witness, but I couldn't help myself.

Glynn's next strategy was to take apart Dr. Howard's CV. Actually, he wanted to decimate it. He went down the list organization by organization and credential by credential and did his best to discredit Dr. Howard.

"Are you a member of the Society of Toxicology?"

"No."

"Are you a member of the American College of Toxicology?"

"No, I am not."

"Are you a member of the European Toxicology Society?"

"No, I am not."

"Are you a member of the European Teratology Society?"

"No, I am not, but if I could just—"

"If the answer is no, just say no."

"In the American system, aren't your teaching credentials really equal to those of an associate professor as opposed to a full professor?"

"It is actually a full faculty member, but yes, that is correct."

"Have you ever taught teratology?"

"I have a number of people who come through the lab who learn how we investigate developmental biology in our laboratory, but we do not have a formal course on teratology in our university, and therefore I have not taught a formal course, so, no."

I looked back over at Liz, who had drawn yet another cartoon of our witness. This time, Dr. Howard had slumped down further in his seat. His curly hair and glasses were only slightly higher than the top of the microphone he was speaking into. At this point I felt sorry for the guy. I really did.

As Glynn moved on to how the Benlate seeped into Donna Castillo's skin, he delivered his final one-two punch. Dr. Howard had calculated that 50 percent of her skin had been exposed when she was sprayed. One simple question unraveled that theory.

"Did you ever attempt to measure that?"

"No. I haven't examined Mrs. Castillo," Dr. Howard said.

Clearly, if less than 50 percent of Donna's skin was exposed, Dr. Howard would have to reduce his calculations, as they were based on the amount of exposed area in square centimeters. Pro rata, that would reduce the total dosage. Glynn also pointed out that Dr. Howard assumed that Donna would not have showered until the next morning, but he hadn't taken into consideration the fact that she might have washed her hands and face, which he agreed would also reduce his numbers.

Glynn drilled down on every last detail, even going so far as to ask whether a substance that could cause cell death at 20 PPB in a petri dish in a laboratory was necessarily a human teratogen.

Dr. Howard's response was that it depended on the substance and what sort of cell, and, of course, the situation. If it was an embryonal cell, which was likely to be killed during a period of vulnerability while the fetus was developing, then it has implications for teratogenicity.

Being a bit smug, Glynn asked if something like caffeine could cause cell death in human lung tissue in a petri dish.

"If you give enough caffeine, I'm sure it could interfere with the metabolism of a cell enough to kill it, just as sugar would," said Dr. Howard.

"Does aspirin do that in a laboratory dish?" asked Glynn.

"I've never experienced that with aspirin, but it is an acid. I would expect if you put it on in sufficient quantity, you will kill cells, yes."

"So the real question is in what dose does the human suffer harm, correct?"

"Yes. The difference between the questions you've been asking and the answer I've been giving is that this actually is known to be a teratogen. The way it works chemically, you would expect it to be a teratogen, and, indeed, in animals we know it is a teratogen."

Glynn's questioning and air of superiority went on for hours. Dr. Howard did what he could, but in the end, he wasn't able to keep up with Glynn as we had hoped.

By the time Glynn finished with Dr. Howard, Liz Russo's cartoon depicted a pathetic man curled up on the stand, his two small eyes behind wire-rimmed glasses barely peeking out over the box. He had taken a real licking up there.

I leaned over to Liz and whispered, "Don't worry—I'll get him back when I redirect."

This was my only chance to resurrect Dr. Howard. He was not a seasoned veteran who could deal with loaded questions like "Is it true that even enough sugar can kill cells?" A novice like Dr. Howard would simply say yes and then live with the implications, whereas a seasoned expert would answer that question by saying, "Enough of anything can kill a cell, but that's not what we're dealing with here. Here we are dealing with very small doses that should not be killing cells." The typical Howard response required redirection, whereas the latter response would not.

My mission on redirect with Dr. Howard was to ask him follow-up questions that would establish the complete and correct answers as opposed to the sound bites that DuPont was seeking to establish. By and large, I thought Dr. Howard did a good job on redirect and replaced the possibly damaging DuPont sound bites with good answers that provided the complete story. When I finished, I felt certain that Dr. Howard's credibility had been successfully restored.

In retrospect, the saddest thing about DuPont's attacks on Dr. Howard was that in reality, he was a scientist who was ahead of his time. DuPont presented their scientific argument as though things could be caused either by genetics or environment, but never both. On the other hand, Dr. Howard very correctly opined to the contrary, stating that most environmental causes work in conjunction with genetics. His opinion was very clear: people have different genetic susceptibility to different environmental toxins. As he would say, some people can smoke four packs of cigarettes a day for forty years and not get lung cancer, whereas others who are more genetically susceptible can develop lung cancer from secondhand smoke. Some people can eat a peanut-butter-and-jelly sandwich every day and be just fine, while others eat a single peanut and drop dead. Genetic susceptibility is widely believed and understood by practically everyone in the world today. But at the time, Dr. Howard was made out to be a heretic for his views at trial, even though what he was saying was generally accepted in the scientific community. This kind of dismissive behavior was typical of DuPont's defense.

# 18

JUST AS I had carefully, methodically, and thoughtfully laid out my case against the defendants, they, too, came in armed with heavy artillery. As expected, their defense plan was to discredit every witness I put on the stand and to dismantle the science that proved Benlate caused Johnny's birth defect. This time, they took aim at Donna Castillo. They tried to shoot holes in every aspect of her testimony about how she was sprayed by Pine Island's machinery. The only issue in play with Donna, however, was her level of exposure. She was bulletproof on all the other elements of her claim. Our tactic was to use whatever evidence we could to support her testimony on this point. We had the weather records for that day, which showed it was hot and windy. The clothes Donna wore, which left the skin on her arms and legs bare, made sense for that kind of weather. And still the defense was determined to do whatever they could to prove otherwise.

They began by asserting that even if Donna had been exposed to Benlate by standing across the street from Pine Island Farms' U-Pick fields that day, there was no real scientific evidence to support the idea that enough of the chemical had reached her to cause the birth defect in her son. Further, they alleged that there was no scientific evidence to back the contention that after their chemical lands on a person's skin, it can seep through the dermis and into the bloodstream to affect a developing embryo or fetus.

The defendants brought in their own spray-drift expert, who showed various wind drift patterns from the two November days in question and how they might have affected Donna as she stood across the street from the farm. Their expert used very impressive computer-generated charts with colorful graphs intimating that the tiny droplets were mostly capable of traveling only a couple of feet—with hardly any of them making it as far as the other side of the street. In this particular expert's opinion, such data made it virtually impossible to believe that Donna could have been sprayed. He shot himself in the foot with his fancy computer charts, however, because if one were to dig deeply enough into his models—which we did—one would easily see that the chemical, when carried by wind, breeze, or air, had the capacity to travel up to half a mile. Naturally, we had the weather reports from the very hour Donna stated she was sprayed to prove our point. And still the defense did their very best to sway the jury into believing Donna was lying—that she never got sprayed by the chemical. Since we had already established the wind and weather patterns earlier, this inconsistency in the expert witness's testimony worked in our favor. I went after him in my cross-examination to point out the obvious.

"Just to be clear, some of this drift will go up to half a mile away, is that correct?" I asked. There was no way he could say no, because he had just spent his entire testimony showing the jury and court the colorful charts that also validated this fact. "A half mile is far. If Donna was one two-hundredth of a half mile away, you're trying to tell this jury that she's not going to get sprayed at any significant level?" I was doing my best to rattle the witness and get the admission I was hoping to hear.

"Uh, well, you see . . ." Their witness fumbled around for an answer that would substantiate his point of view, but the reality was, there wasn't one.

"Tell me something: How can you be so sure she didn't get sprayed? Are you also a weatherman? A meteorologist?" I taunted him with these types of questions because what he was asking the jury to believe was nothing more than voodoo science. It was bullshit. We unraveled his testimony and set the jury straight on this point.

As mentioned earlier, when we went to trial, my two key witnesses had never testified in court before. That's an extremely risky situation for a plaintiff's lawyer. In this case, my first witness was the plaintiff herself, who was exposed to the chemical. The only witness to this exposure was her infant daughter, who couldn't testify because she was too young to remember what happened and had nothing to say that would add value to the case. My second key witness was my lynchpin expert, Dr. Howard. To prepare for trial, I had to work repeatedly with both witnesses, because it's extremely common for first-timers to get tense and freeze up. Even a seasoned professional witness might have been nervous under the circumstances in that courtroom. A witness must still perform, however, or there's a price to pay. No matter how much practice one puts in prior to trial, one's testimony on game day is the only thing that truly counts.

Unlike the so-called wind-drift expert I had just taken to school on the stand and the two novices I had prepared as witnesses for our side, there were some witnesses who, by virtue of experience, were considered rock-star witnesses. DuPont had brought in one such superstar expert, Dr. Robert Brent, the self-proclaimed "King of Teratology" who I mentioned earlier. To this day, Dr. Brent is one of the finest expert witnesses I have ever cross-examined. He had been giving expert witness testimony for forty years—longer than I had been alive at the time. He had given testimony in at least forty trials and given hundreds of depositions between the time he first took the stand and our case. Dr. Brent was good—*really* good. He was smooth and unflappable, and came across as very knowledgeable. As their key expert witness, Dr. Brent could have been the guy who won the case for DuPont if I hadn't stopped him.

Dr. Brent was a full-time member of Alfred I. duPont Institute (at the Nemours Alfred I. duPont Hospital for Children in Wilmington, Delaware) and the Jefferson Medical College (now known as the Sidney Kimmel Medical College) of Thomas Jefferson University in Philadelphia. It's important to note that the DuPont Institute has no relation to the DuPont company, except that in 1916 Alfred I. duPont left the DuPont company after shareholders voted to remove him from the board of directors. Upon Alfred's death in 1935, the Alfred I. duPont Testamentary Trust was created, with the Nemours Foundation (created in 1936) as sole beneficiary. Foundation funds were used in 1940 to establish the Alfred I. duPont Institute and the Hospital for Children. The relationship between Dr. Brent and the hospital was formed in the late 1980s when the dean of the medical school came to him with the news that his research center was to be destroyed to make room for an eleven-story building the college was planning to put on the same grounds. While Dr. Brent searched for a new location to house his laboratories, the dean suggested he move his lab and all of his researchers to a new facility constructed in the old children's hospital and create an educational program for residents and medical students.

While Dr. Brent often referred to himself as the King of Teratology, he had no board certification in the discipline. His self-proclaimed title comes from his passionate study of teratology, which was the area in which he spent most of his time working. He considered himself to be a toxicologist, but only insofar as toxicology pertained to teratology. He also had no certificate or license—nor was he a member of any society or organization—for epidemiology. Dr. Brent thought himself to be a qualified geneticist and pediatrician, but he was not a qualified obstetrician. When asked during his deposition about his intentions as an expert witness in the trial, he was clear to state that his purpose would be to rebut the opinions of the geneticists, obstetricians, toxicologists, and epidemiologists we put on the stand as witnesses. In his opinion, he was a qualified expert in at least five specialties.

Given his accomplishments, Dr. Brent was asked to contribute content in the areas of toxicology and the law in a book by Dr. Anthony R. Scialli entitled *A Clinical Guide to Reproductive and Developmental Toxicology*. Dr. Brent contributed a chapter called "The Ingredients of a Lawsuit." I thought this was an interesting title, coming from a guy who got paid to testify in defense of chemical companies.

When I asked him about this experience, he acknowledged having contributed to the publication but had no recollection of ever talking to Dr. Scialli about the book or the process of writing it. Interestingly, in the book Dr. Brent again claimed to be a toxicologist, epidemiologist, geneticist, pediatrician, and teratologist—a slight overstatement of his credentials at the time. And though Dr. Brent had no recall of his experience, the first person Dr. Scialli mentioned in the acknowledgments of the book was Dr. Brent. It seemed peculiar for an author to so prominently thank someone who had no memory of working on the book. Usually, that type of acknowledgment is reserved for someone who contributed a great deal to the process, not just the writing of a single chapter. I pointed this out during the trial to establish the concept that Dr. Brent may have suffered from a convenient memory—choosing very carefully what he could and could not recall for the purposes of a trial.

Dr. Brent had testified that most chemicals are known to be teratogens in humans if the dose is high enough. In his experience, he had never seen lists of human teratogens compiled by different scientists that were identical. He said it was difficult to figure out teratogenic doses in humans because chemicals are more difficult to regulate, and the size of dose needed to be harmful is more challenging to ascertain with chemicals than with drugs. The determination of what constitutes harmful exposure or a harmful dose of a certain chemical can be made only through animal studies and the reports of investigators in the field from the EPA, the National Institute of Environmental Health Sciences, and the Centers for Disease Control and Prevention. It was his belief that scientists in the field have greater expertise and are in better positions to make informed, intelligent recommendations than the manufacturers of specific chemicals. He went so far as to say that a major multinational company such as DuPont isn't always in the best position to warn users of its products' potential dangers because it depends on its personnel. Of course, when pressed on cross-examination, he also felt it was ludicrous for the EPA to have more knowledge about products than the manufacturers of those products.

It turned out that Dr. Brent had known Dr. Staples for more than thirty years. He had learned about Staples's research on benomyl and had done two consultations for DuPont, including work on the 1980 Staples study. He certainly had a lot of familiarity with the product, the research, the studies, and the potential impact of exposure to Benlate. Dr. Brent disagreed with the findings of the 1980 Staples rat study and was well aware that the EPA had considered warning pregnant women about exposure to Benlate. He was also aware of the rebuttable presumption placed on DuPont, which had been lifted after the 1982 Staples study. Despite our discovery to the contrary, Dr. Brent testified that the methodology of both Staples studies was the same. When I pushed him a little harder on the validity of the Staples studies, he said he could be persuaded to change his opinion about whether they were sound, solid studies that followed proper methodology.

While Dr. Brent believed the Hoogenboom study supported the 1982 Staples study, he admitted that most subsequent studies didn't clearly determine whether there were no-effect levels and started out at the 62.5-milligram dose level. He believed that a better study than the ones in existence would focus only on activity on the ninth day of gestation, because that was when microphthalmia could occur. The ninth day of gestation was the most sensitive day in rats for eye and lung formation, as well as for possible development of hydrocephalus, encephalocele, congenital heart disease, absent kidneys, and vertebral malformations, among other worrisome conditions. The most sensitive organ developing on the ninth day is the brain, and the eye is technically part of the brain. Any study that tested benomyl on rats exposed between day four and seven would not result in microphthalmia. In order to see this malformation, the rat had to be exposed between days nine and eleven. The eyes don't stop developing for quite some time, and neither does the brain, so vigilance thereafter is important, too. What Dr. Brent was sure of was that if benomyl crossed the placenta in rats, then it crossed the placenta in humans. As long as a compound is in the mother's blood and it gets to the placenta, it will get to the embryo or fetus.

Dr. Brent stated in his testimony that he had no doubt Johnny Castillo's microphthalmia occurred within the proper time frame for a toxic agent to have produced it. He also had no doubt that the alleged exposure occurred during the critical period of Johnny's eye development.

Although Dr. Brent said he wasn't in a position to comment on whether Dr. Howard was unqualified to testify, he had no reason to believe he wasn't. In fact, Dr. Brent thought Dr. Howard was qualified but wrong. For this reason, he did his best to discredit Dr. Howard's testimony and credentials, especially his in vitro studies and his calculations regarding Donna's exposure. However, in a chemotherapeutic setting, the in vitro tests determined exactly what Dr. Van Velzen had with exposure to benomyl, finding whether and when cell death occurs. The tests would confirm his findings. Dr. Brent also testified that he agreed that a genetic expert could not prove a genetic cause, and that Johnny and his family had undergone all the state-of-the-art tests available and the results had all come back negative. Although Dr. Brent couldn't say with a reasonable degree of medical certainty what caused Johnny's microphthalmia, he couldn't rule out an environmental factor such as benomyl exposure (which he considered a "very remote possibility"). Despite his own testimony that he had no right to say within a reasonable degree of medical certainty that Johnny's condition was recessive-inherited, X-linked recessive, or new-dominant recessive, and that every genetic test done on the Castillos came back negative, Dr. Brent still personally believed genetics was the most likely cause. Given the facts, I had no idea what the basis of this opinion was. I could fathom only that it was meant to confuse the jury and dissuade them from the thought that the cause might have been benomyl.

What Dr. Brent did say was that every proven chemical or drug teratogen results in multiple malformations, and benomyl was a proven teratogen in rats. But he also believed that the rats had multiple malformations along with microphthalmia in the studies that had been done. In fact, he believed that all the fetuses born with abnormal eyes in the Staples studies also had growth retardation. In reality, it was clear from the studies' underlying data that multiple malformations occurred only with very high doses of benomyl, and single malformations occurred with lower doses. Yet while Dr. Brent believed that humans could experience a teratogenic effect from benomyl, he also believed that effect would only come at doses higher than humans have the capability of being exposed to.

When I asked Dr. Brent if he knew what those doses would be, he said he couldn't calculate a dose of benomyl that would result in a teratogenic effect in a human fetus because he would need response curves and blood levels. He did say all chemicals in the blood supply would circulate through both the fetal blood supply and the entire blood supply of a pregnant woman. On cross-examination, Dr. Brent admitted, after having reviewed DuPont's papers on dermal and inhalation exposure based on the company's own data and data from the World Health Organization (WHO), that he believed 10 to 15 percent of the amount of the chemical applied to the skin would get into the human bloodstream. This testimony was great for the Castillos.

"Do you believe that, based on Donna Castillo's exposure, benomyl could have gotten into her bloodstream?" I asked.

"Yes, some would have gotten into her bloodstream; however, a very small proportion. Her absorption rate was probably less than ten to fifteen percent, because it was a windy day and it dried on her skin," Dr. Brent responded. His estimation was up to five times higher than the 3 percent rate we were using. That fact fit perfectly with Johnny's low-dose exposure and his having only a single malformation to make the ideal picture we were hoping to create for the case.

When I pushed Dr. Brent about how he could possibly know this, he admitted that he wasn't in a position to testify about the rate of benomyl absorption into Donna's bloodstream, but he still believed humans have lower absorption rates than rats, because humans have thicker skin.

As it turned out, Dr. Brent had to admit he was not an expert on dermal exposure. In fact, he had never written a published work or given a seminar or presentation on benomyl or its potential teratogenic effects. He had never conducted a study looking for reproductive toxicity in humans or rats with benomyl, either.

Though Dr. Brent was tough, I did my best to challenge his expertise and authority. It wasn't easy, and in fact it got a bit ugly at times, but in the end I had a good feeling that I had managed to do more than just rattle his cage—I clearly established that at least 3 percent of the Benlate Donna had been exposed to got into her bloodstream.

That was big.

# 19

THE QUESTIONABLE TACTICS the defense engaged in from the outset of the trial continued right through the very last witness's testimony. DuPont, Pine Island Farms, and their combined counsel had
no respect for the court-set deadlines and repeatedly took advantage
of Judge Donner's liberal procedures. From the start, I also had to
endure endless disparaging comments about Limogate from Glynn.
Whenever he could, he'd sneak in such snide remarks as "Judge, I
don't know if Mr. Ferraro will be here for the end of the trial, because
he's defending criminal charges" and "Jim's got enough investigations
to deal with because of his limo situation." He took advantage of every
opportunity to mention the subject in the presence of the judge, who
soon became as fed up with it as I was. Fortunately, it wasn't the type
of commentary Glynn could direct toward the jury to affect our case.

Gaebe's dirty tricks were just as bad. During Lynn Chaffin's testimony, he said he had offers from people to lie on behalf of Pine Island
Farms. When pressed to divulge who would make such an offer, Chaffin mentioned that one of the offers had come from Sonya Sipes of

LaBelle Plant World, a supplier to the farm. Sonya had worked at LaBelle Plant World since June 1992 as an assistant comptroller. As a result of Chaffin's revelation, I felt the need to call Sonya as a last-minute witness.

Gaebe, Kleinberg, and Glynn all objected to my request, suggesting it was an attempt to rebut Chaffin's testimony as an adverse witness, but it wasn't. The defense never anticipated Chaffin was going to make such an outlandish statement at trial—but he did. This was put on as part of their defense and was elicited by farm counsel. Pretty stupid. It was a lame attempt by Pine Island Farms to show that Chaffin wouldn't lie or support lying, when in fact he was a proven liar based on his cell phone records. Glynn did his best to deny that that was what Chaffin said, while Gaebe and Kleinberg tried to paint it as mere mischaracterization by Chaffin that someone had offered to lie on his behalf. Judge Donner heard the arguments from all sides and ruled that Ms. Sipes could testify.

My firm subpoenaed invoices and contracts related to Pine Island Farms from LaBelle Plant World for December 1995, which Sipes said was the time she first became aware of the lawsuit between the Castillos and the defendants. It was her job to provide all their documentation to us. No one else was involved in providing those documents to any of the parties connected to the litigation. During her testimony, Sipes said she had spoken with Gaebe about these invoices, and that he had also asked for copies. Gaebe had conducted a phone deposition with her, and she had also received a call from him the day before she was called to testify.

I wanted to cut to the chase, so I asked her the most obvious question. "Ms. Sipes, have you ever offered to lie on behalf of Pine Island Farms with regard to this lawsuit?"

Gaebe objected to my question on the basis of relevancy, foundation, and that it was beyond the scope of rebuttal. But the judge had already ruled on that before allowing the witness to take the stand.

"Overruled," Judge Donner said.

"Definitely not," Sipes said in answer.

"Do you know Lynn Chaffin?" I asked.

"I don't know him personally. I've only heard his name through the process of this lawsuit. The first time I heard his name was December 1995. We have never spoken," Sipes testified.

"And when was the last time you had contact with any lawyers from Pine Island Farms prior to today?"

"Yesterday afternoon. I received two phone calls: one from Greg Gaebe and the other from Jack Wishart."

Gaebe objected, but Judge Donner overruled, allowing Sipes to testify about the purpose of those two calls.

"Gaebe basically asked me if I would tell him why I was coming to court, and reminded me to tell the truth. He basically kept guessing why I was coming. I told him nothing and said I didn't want to discuss it. About an hour after that call, Jack Wishart called and told me he was the grower for Pine Island Farms. He, too, wanted [to] remind me to tell the truth, and he felt I knew nothing about the facts of the case. He said the other side was losing and there was nothing I could say in this case that would hurt their side. He said Gaebe might call me again and wanted me to know he was a nice man."

"And when was the first time you've spoken to me, Ms. Sipes?" I asked.

"This morning."

I had no further questions.

Gaebe got his chance to cross-examine Sonya Sipes, but he wasn't able to intimidate her or find any flaws in her story. Her testimony left a lot of room for doubt about Chaffin's and Wishart's credibility, if not the integrity of the entire Pine Island Farm legal team.

One of the last witnesses to testify in the case was Dr. Brad Pollock, an associate professor and the director of the department of epidemiology at the University of Florida in Gainesville. His area of expertise was in pediatric epidemiology. He testified for us in a rebuttal case, as did Sonya Sipes.

Epidemiological studies are designed to determine the cause and distribution of disease in populations, with the goal of identifying risk factors for disease as well as potential protective means to reduce the occurrence of disease. While there are several different types of epidemiological studies, the bulk of the studies conducted are observational studies. These are studies in which people who have been exposed to some sort of disease are observed so researchers can learn more about the subsequent outcome of the disease. In many ways, observational studies are randomized, because no one is actually being subjected to some sort of potentially dangerous disease or noxious agent; researchers are merely watching a segment of the population that has already been exposed to such a disease or agent in order to witness and better understand the subsequent effects. There are a number of subcategories of observational studies that can be ranked in order of how much evidence they provide in explaining the causes of a particular type of disease or condition. Some examples of these subcategories include cohort studies (also called prospective studies), case control studies, ecological studies, and cross-sectional surveys.

Having the findings of an ecological study—one in which disease occurrence is measured by exposure within an aggregate grouping of people—was extremely relevant to our case. The example that Dr. Pollock gave on the stand involved a study that looked at the rate of childhood leukemia in the state of Florida by examining geographic units like Dade County, Alachua County, and Broward County and comparing rates of leukemia occurrence. While such a study doesn't provide information on what an individual's actual exposure to a disease may be, it does allow scientists to make an assessment based on a geographic grouping of people.

Dr. Pollock read about an attempt to conduct this type of study with regard to the relationship between benomyl exposure and incidence rates of microphthalmia and anophthalmia in Italy known as the Spagnolo Study. In the simplest terms, the researchers got information about how much benomyl was sold in the region under examination and then looked at the acreage therein to reach some conclusions about exposure levels. In addition, the scientists looked at data on the occupations of the parents and birth defect records that indicated one or both parents were involved in the agricultural industry, along with information about the rate of occurrence of anophthalmia in various regions. Dr. Spagnolo's study pointed out that there was no possible way (nor was any attempt made) to conduct an ecological study on pregnant women who were exposed to benomyl at critical points in their pregnancy. In other words, this study was meaningless to both the Castillos and the defendants. It proved literally nothing.

This was an essential point to drive home one last time in the trial, as DuPont had consistently pointed out that there had been no epidemiological studies to support our case. There were none to support their defense either.

When I asked Dr. Pollock if the types of studies an epidemiologist conducts would allow him to determine whether benomyl or Benlate causes microphthalmia in children like Johnny Castillo, he said there was very little information that would allow him to draw a conclusion. In other words, there were no adequate epidemiological studies that could show or not show that benomyl was a factor in causing microphthalmia. That makes sense, because of the impossibility of locating random pregnant women around the globe who were conclusively exposed to benomyl and then gave birth to children with microphthalmia.

Epidemiological studies are not conclusive on their own. The various pieces can point to what is going on, but they are not a substitute for laboratory testing because they are observational; they cannot provide the definitive conclusions obtained with animal studies, toxicological testing, or pathological testing to determine whether benomyl causes microphthalmia.

I was completely satisfied that Dr. Pollock put to rest any concerns the defense raised about our case not having epidemiological studies once and for all. Those kinds of studies were clearly not applicable. And with this final declaration, I was able to feel good about the rest of the science we had presented throughout the four and a half weeks of testimony.

Glynn did a brief cross-examination before Gaebe passed on his chance and I followed up with a short redirect. Once we were through, we rested our case.

The court recessed for a one-hour lunch. Judge Donner was very clear that she wanted to start again precisely at 1:00 p.m., because there were a lot of housekeeping items to take care of upon our return and she wanted to adjourn no later than 5:30.

As is customary, the attorneys gathered in the courtroom before the jury to go over the matters at hand. First on Gaebe's docket were motions on behalf of Pine Island Farms to move the court for a curative instruction (which is when the judge addresses the jury in order to negate the prejudicial effect of an inappropriate argument or improperly offered evidence) and to declare a mistrial on the basis of the testimony of Sonya Sipes. The reason he gave was that her testimony had "absolutely nothing to do with any definition of rebuttal in any court of law." Sipes had been asked questions about communications between her and Gaebe and her and Jack Wishart, which she answered truthfully, providing the court with an account of the instructions or requests she received from Gaebe as well as Mr. Wishart to come in, cooperate, and tell the truth. Gaebe felt her testimony was prejudicial and inflammatory only insofar as she testified that Wishart made a statement the day before her testimony that "Pine Island Farms is winning."

I was floored.

What did he want the judge to say?

That Pine Island Farms was *not* winning?

Personally, I thought it was a flattering statement. I didn't see any prejudice to the testimony at all, and actually found Gaebe's objection interesting from a strategic point of view. I was trying to think of a reason why he might want a curative instruction about his side winning. It was such an odd move on Gaebe's part, and one that didn't pay off. The judge didn't like it any more than I did. She denied the motion for curative instruction, and the motion for a mistrial.

We spent the next hour bickering over the admissible evidence everyone still had to introduce before jury deliberation began. Judge Donner was being quite generous with all the lawyers, allowing the defendants and plaintiff each to be comfortable with what we had in evidence. One by one, Glynn, Chumbley, Gaebe, and Kleinberg had their turn to go back and forth on items they either did or did not want admitted. Liz Russo argued for the relevance of using fertilizer records from 1988, '89, and '90 to establish chemical purchasing patterns, which had been questioned in terms of relevance despite testimony about planting patterns and when fertilizer is used.

"Is that it?" Judge Donner asked as we got to the last piece of the evidence.

"One other thing," I said, sounding a bit like Lieutenant Columbo just before he was about to solve a big case. "Mr. Gaebe's exhibits: he's got blowups of testimony, but some of them are not really testimony. [They're] just objections back and forth by counsel." I had no idea whether Gaebe knew he did this—if it was intentional or he just thought he could get away with it—but there was no way in hell I wasn't going to call him out on this incredibly low and unprofessional behavior.

"First of all, objections of counsel do not go into anybody's evidence," Judge Donner clearly stated. She wasn't very happy with where this was headed. You see, whenever a lawyer believes the rules of evidence have been broken during testimony, he may shout, "Objection, move to strike." If the judge sustains the objection, the testimony is deemed improper and is stricken from consideration by the jury. Whether or not Gaebe was consciously trying to sneak some of the remarks most advantageous to his defense back into play through these boards, the judge was not having any of it.

Gaebe tried to explain his way out of this by suggesting I had it all wrong. "What he's talking about is the evidence in this case, and we were in a sidebar when he made this objection. Now, you know it's easy for Mr. Ferraro to say he has some colloquy and objections. The fact of the matter is, he's given you an incomplete representation of what's in that thing. This is classic Ferraro, okay?"

But you have to know Judge Donner was smarter than that. "Excuse me. Let me see if I can get this straight, because maybe I'm missing something. You need to answer just one question. Is this trial transcript?" she asked Gaebe.

"Yes."

"Is that sidebar?"

"No . . . but . . ." Gaebe had been busted.

His boards included not only references to objections but also sidebar conversations. Those were most definitely off-limits to jurors.

"Thereupon the proceedings were had . . ." and "We went back . . ." were just two examples of how the "evidence" written on the boards began. They were clearly referring to sidebar conversations. "You are *not* having sidebar before the jury," Judge Donner said firmly, practically scolding Gaebe.

"I agree. I agree." He was doing his best to backpedal.

The judge continued. "That is ridiculous. I am just shocked. That is classic Gaebe, but I am shocked that you would try to put a sidebar in front of this jury. So you go back and you review your material. If it is sidebar, don't try to show it. That is the reason you have something called a sidebar, Mr. Gaebe."

I was quick to point out how many of them I had counted. "I have ten of these, Your Honor. Can I show you the next page?"

"I don't care about your next page."

"I wasn't going to call their attention to that part. That wasn't the thing I was going to show the jury . . ." Gaebe lamely offered in self-defense.

"Forget call to their attention. You are not going to show that at all."

This sidebar sideshow had turned into a courtroom shit show. Kleinberg was embarrassed enough to stand up and assure the judge they wouldn't use the boards at all, they'd simply read from the transcripts. As long as they didn't read anything from the sidebars or colloquy between counsel and the court, I had no objection.

Of course, I also needed to point out that they couldn't read anything that had been overruled in an objection from their transcript, either, as I suspected they'd try to get away with that, too. I wanted to say, "C'mon, fellas, where's your dignity?" But I didn't have to. The judge clocked them pretty good.

Once we got through the final few issues we needed to review before closing arguments, Judge Donner gave us her instructions on how she expected it to go down. I was to go first, with ninety minutes to give my closing. Mr. Gaebe would go next, followed by Mr. Kleinberg and then Mr. Glynn. I would then be allowed one more opportunity to finish up with my rebuttal.

Glynn attempted to persuade the judge to allow a five-minute break between Pine Island Farms' counsel's closing argument and his own, which she declined. She had never allowed such a thing before, and wasn't about to start now.

The courtroom was packed with people and members of the media, complete with cameras, lights, and cables everywhere. They were all present to witness the historic outcome. It was standing room only while we waited for the jury to come back into the courtroom. David Lipman, an accomplished trial lawyer and colleague of mine, was eager to see the conclusion of the trial and came to watch the closing arguments. He walked over to say hello minutes before I was about to start. I talked to him about the previous night's Miami Heat game, which bewildered Lipman. In fact, Lipman called me right after the trial expressing his awe that I could talk about a basketball game just minutes before closing such a complex case. When I am totally prepared to close a case, a certain calm comes over me. I was ready.

Judge Donner instructed her clerk, Ray, to bring the jury back into the courtroom to commence closing arguments. It had been a long four and a half weeks for everyone. The jury shuffled in and made their way to the jury box.

"Counsel, the jury is coming in," Ray announced.

"You may be seated. Is the plaintiff ready to proceed?" Judge Donner asked, turning to me.

"Yes, Your Honor."

"Is the defendant DuPont ready to proceed?"

"Yes, Your Honor," said Glynn.

"Is the defendant Pine Island Farms ready to proceed?"

"Yes, Your Honor," said Gaebe.

"The court is ready. You may proceed."

Tensions were high, and my adrenaline was pumping.

I stood up from behind the table where I had sat for the last six weeks and looked around the courtroom. I grabbed my yellow legal pad from the table to use for reference, though I knew exactly what I was going to say. I had gone through this closing in my head over and over. I slowly walked toward the jury and made eye contact with as many jurors as I could. I glanced behind me to find my ten-year-old son, James, in the crowd. He had come to watch his old man during closing arguments. Seeing his sweet, innocent face in the courtroom was so meaningful to me. Every dad wants to be a superhero to his kid, and this was my chance to show James what I did in the world—how I fought the evil powers to protect people's rights for the good of us all.

The other important person in the courtroom that day was Johnny Castillo. By design, I had asked John to be present during opening statements and closing arguments. Several colleagues had tried to persuade me to put him on the stand, but I didn't see the value in having this young blind boy testify. While I had the right to do so, it just didn't feel tasteful or appropriate to me. It was far less intrusive for Johnny and his family to have the jury watch the day-in-the-life video we had made, which was much more powerful for the jury to experience. I also knew that sometimes these types of cases aren't well served by overexposing the plaintiff. I certainly didn't want the jury to be turned off in some way—or, worse, to be desensitized by seeing the boy in the courtroom every day. Having him there with us now during this pivotal moment meant so much more, and would likely have greater impact.

"Good afternoon, ladies and gentlemen. I know it's been a long haul for you. This is now your fifth week in this courtroom, and we appreciate your time and effort. It's a huge responsibility to be a juror on a case like this, or any other case, and you've done a great job of fulfilling it. It's your determination that decides what is right and fair under the law.

"We're here to determine liability and damages. We are not in this courtroom for sympathy. I will go through each element of the liability and damages in this case.

"In a broad sense, we all know what this case is about. It's about defendant Pine Island Farms using the Benlate product that was made by the defendant DuPont, which was sprayed on that lady sitting right over there six to seven weeks into her pregnancy and affected her little boy sitting right next to her.

"While the defenses will be many, there is one overriding thing we need to look at: Is it a coincidence that Johnny Castillo's eyes stopped developing or arrested in their development six to seven weeks into the pregnancy at the same time his mom was exposed to Benlate? That is the one overriding factor in this case to keep in mind when we go through the evidence. When we are finished with closing arguments, which is our interpretation of the evidence, you will retire to the jury room and you will have instructions that Judge Donner will give you."

Although I spent the bulk of my ninety minutes going through and reviewing the science of the case, restating the facts to be sure the jury agreed that DuPont and Pine Island Farms were liable, what I also needed the jury to understand was how to calculate damages. One part of that calculation is easy—that's the economic consideration, including the cost of schooling, vocational training, lifelong medical treatment, and day-to-day care for Johnny. The harder part would be getting them to comprehend and assess the noneconomic damages, such as pain and suffering or loss of comfort and support. Explaining to a jury how to value something of that magnitude isn't easy. A lot of lawyers pull a number out of the air and hope it sticks. Those numbers, however, are usually random—there is no rational basis or formula used to justify that number. One of the many things my background as a CPA taught me, though, is that numbers become less abstract and are more meaningful to people when they have some sort of connotation to them.

I believe it is my job to provide the jury with an equation or formula so they can reasonably calculate the proper amount of monetary damages. I suggest looking at life in units of time, because everything we do is measured that way. We quantify our sleep, work, play, meals, travel—literally everything we do—in units of time. I use examples of time and compensation the jury can easily comprehend, such as the salaries of a schoolteacher or police officer; and I am always sure to throw in an expert witness who has testified. Typically, I pick the pay rate of the scummiest witness presented by the defense without naming him to the jury. In this case, I thought it was Dr. Brent. I used his rate of pay as an expert witness of $750 an hour and said that if the witness spent one hundred hours preparing and testifying in the case, he or she would be entitled to $75,000 for his or her time. Once a jury hears that, I ask them to consider someone like Johnny Castillo and his circumstances and compare them to the teacher, police officer, or expert witness.

"What is Johnny's job?" I asked the jury. "Johnny's job is to live life—an entire life—with no eyes. His job was given to him by DuPont. He doesn't have the option of quitting, retiring, or refusing to continue that job. He has to live with that job for the rest of his life."

I went on to explain that despite the fact that he has no eyes, his life expectancy isn't likely to be impaired. There is certainly no reason to believe it will be significantly shorter than that of a healthy, sighted person. The life expectancy tables showed that Johnny had at least seventy more years to live in a job he never asked to have. The number I put out there was somewhere between twenty and thirty dollars per hour for Johnny, with a midrange of twenty-five dollars per hour. It seemed irrational, if not downright insulting, to believe this was an unfair figure to expect the jury to agree to when deciding damages. What they had to do in this case was consider the bodily injury sustained by John Castillo and any resulting pain and suffering, disability, physical impairment, disfigurement, mental anguish, inconvenience, and loss of capacity to enjoy life he had experienced since birth or would experience throughout his future. The jury also had to consider the reasonable value of medical care, hospitalization, and nursing, as well as any other practicable treatment necessary for Johnny, along with any loss of ability to earn money once he reached the age of eighteen.

Juan and Donna Castillo were also entitled to damages in the form of the reasonable value or expense of hospitalization, medical care, nursing, and necessary or reasonable treatment for their child until Johnny reached the age of eighteen, as well as for loss of companionship, society, love, affection, and solace in the past and in the future due to their child's injury. I asked for somewhere between five and ten dollars per hour for their pain and suffering, loss of affection, and solace. With our strong rationale and numbers in such a reasonable range, how could a jury not respond favorably?

The total damages we were pursuing in this case were in the general range of $20 to $30 million. Based on our assessment, that was a fair number to award the Castillos. This general range was what I refer to as my playing field. Whenever I win a case, the award usually falls somewhere in that playing field.

I told the jury that, according to our calculations, $25 million was the amount that took into account all the aforementioned considerations, but they could go higher or lower, or choose their own formula if it was better than the formula I had proposed. Further, I challenged my opponents to present a better formula than mine. If they did, I told the jury they should use that formula over mine. I am not a lawyer who just picks numbers out of thin air. I understand that without a meaningful explanation, the jury is less likely to accept your numbers. I answer all the questions and concerns I can possibly anticipate when I lay out a formula the way I do.

Although I thought I had done a really good job throughout the trial, there was still that one juror who left a seed of doubt that we would take this all the way home. I knew the other jurors got it, but I had my concerns about him. Still, I had no regrets, no fear that I had missed something along the way. I was prepared to live with the result. Now all I had to do was wait and see what DuPont and Pine Island Farms were going to say in their closing arguments.

Counsel for Pine Island Farms spent the bulk of their allotted time talking about when they spray their fields and what their planting patterns are, and overstating how they primarily bought chemicals such as Benlate from a different supplier than the one we had records for. Of course, they liked the supplier whose records had all been destroyed by Hurricane Andrew, because with no records it's hard to prove anything had been bought in the time frame in question.

As expected, DuPont attacked the science and the caliber of our witnesses.

I did what I could in my rebuttal to combat the positions both defendants had taken not only throughout the trial but also now in their last-ditch efforts during closing arguments. I made a point of saying to the jury that no one came in for the defense and did any testing the way we had done with Dr. Van Velzen. They could have done the same thing we did, but chose not to. Instead, they relied on previous studies, most of which weren't necessarily in their favor.

We finished closing arguments in time to meet Judge Donner's request to adjourn by 5:30 p.m. that Wednesday night. It had been a long haul for everyone. And now it would become a nail-biting waiting game to see who won the credibility war with the jury.

# 20

ON THE MORNING of June 6, 1996, the jury was ushered into the courtroom just as they had been every other morning for the previous five weeks. Only this morning was different. On this morning, Judge Donner handed them copies of the jury charge. It was as if she had given them a pop quiz, except they had known it was coming.

"Remember back in high school when your teacher said, 'Don't turn over your paper until I tell you'? Well, this is one of those papers. I will tell you when to turn it over, and then you will follow along with me. Are we all together here?" Judge Donner said as though she were addressing a classroom instead of a courtroom.

"All right, then. Members of the jury, turn over your papers and begin reading with me on the second page. I shall now instruct you on the law that you must follow in reaching your verdict. It is your duty as jurors to decide the issues, and *only* those issues, that I submit for determination by your verdict. In reaching your verdict, you should consider and weigh the evidence, decide the disputed issues of fact, and apply the law on which I shall instruct you to the facts as you find them from the evidence.

"The evidence in this case consists of the sworn testimony of the witnesses, all exhibits received in evidence, and all facts that may be admitted or agreed to by the parties. In determining the facts, you may draw reasonable inferences from the evidence. You may make deductions and reach conclusions that your common sense leads you to draw from the facts shown by the evidence in this case. But you should not speculate on any matters outside the evidence.

"In determining the believability of any witness and the weight to be given their testimony, you may properly consider the demeanor of the witness while testifying; the frankness or lack of frankness of the witness; the intelligence of the witness; any interest the witness may have in the outcome of the case; the means and opportunity the witness had to know facts about which the witness testified; the ability of the witness to remember the matters about which the witness testified; and the reasonableness of the testimony of the witness, considered in the light of all the evidence in the case and in the light of your experience and common sense.

"You may accept opinion testimony on certain technical subjects, reject it, or give it the weight you think it deserves, considering the knowledge, skill, experience, training, or education of the witness; the reasons given by the witness for the opinion expressed; and all the other evidence in the case.

"In your deliberations, you are to consider several distinct claims. First, plaintiffs allege that defendant DuPont placed Benlate on the market in an unreasonably dangerous condition. The plaintiffs also allege that defendant DuPont was negligent in the design, testing, and sale of Benlate. Finally, plaintiffs assert that Pine Island Farms was negligent in its use of Benlate. Plaintiffs claim that as a result of the actions of the defendants, plaintiffs suffered damage. Both defendants deny the plaintiffs' claims. Although these claims have been tried together, each is separate from the others, and each party is entitled to have you consider the evidence as it relates to each claim separately, as if each claim were tried before you separately.

"Now, the plaintiffs have two claims against the defendant DuPont. The first issue to consider and determine is whether the Benlate sold by defendant DuPont was defective when it left the possession of DuPont, and if so, whether such defect was a legal cause of loss, injury, or damage sustained by the plaintiffs. A product is defective if by reason of its design the product is in a condition unreasonably dangerous to consumers, users, or bystanders, and the product is expected to and does reach the user without substantial change affecting that condition. A product is unreasonably dangerous because of its design if the product fails to perform as safely as an ordinary consumer, user, or bystander would expect when used as intended or in a manner reasonably foreseeable by the manufacturer, or the risk of danger in the design outweighs the benefits.

"If the greater weight of the evidence does not support this claim of the plaintiffs, your verdict should be for the defendant DuPont. However, if the greater weight of the evidence does support this claim, then your verdict should be for the plaintiffs.

"The issue on the second claim of the plaintiffs against DuPont is whether DuPont was negligent in the design, testing, or sale of Benlate, and if so, whether such negligence was a legal cause of the loss, injury, or damage sustained by the plaintiffs.

"If the greater weight of the evidence does not support this claim of the plaintiffs, your verdict should be for the defendant DuPont. However, if the greater weight of the evidence does support this claim, then your verdict should be for the plaintiffs.

"The absence of a pregnancy or birth defect warning on the product label is not a basis of liability.

"In determining whether Benlate was defectively designed and whether the risk of danger in design outweighs the benefits of Benlate, you may consider the usefulness and desirability of the Benlate product, the availability of other and safer products to meet the same needs, the likelihood of injury and its probable seriousness, the obviousness of danger, common knowledge and normal public expectations of danger, and the avoidability of injury by care in use of the product.

"Okay, now we get to the issues for your determination on the negligence claim of the plaintiffs against defendant Pine Island Farms. One, whether Pine Island Farms sprayed Benlate at the subject field on November first or November second, 1989; two, whether Pine Island Farms was negligent in the spraying of Benlate on November first or second, 1989; and if so, whether such negligence was a legal cause of loss, injury, or damage sustained by the plaintiffs.

"If the greater weight of the evidence does not support this claim of the plaintiffs, your verdict should be for the defendant Pine Island Farms. However, if the greater weight of the evidence does support this claim, then your verdict should be for the plaintiffs.

"Negligence is the failure to use reasonable care. Reasonable care is that degree of care that a reasonably careful person would use under like circumstances. Negligence may consist either in doing something that a reasonably careful person would not do under like circumstances or in failing to do something that a reasonably careful person would do under like circumstances."

Judge Donner continued to explain in very easy-to-understand terms each and every claim and the evidence the jury should or should not consider when making their determination for a verdict and damages. If they found for both defendants, they were not responsible for considering any damages. However, if they found for the plaintiffs against either or both defendants, they were instructed to award an amount of money that the greater weight of the evidence showed would fairly and adequately compensate them for such loss, injury, or damage, including any such damage as the plaintiffs were reasonably certain to incur or experience in the future.

This wasn't going to be a complete slam dunk for the Castillos, but I felt we had laid out a really good and convincing argument and a relatively easy formula to help the jury calculate damages if they agreed that the Castillos were due monetary compensation. This was a big and important case—one that wasn't important only to my clients but also important to the planet. We were asking for big money, somewhere around $25 million in damages. Whether we would get the full amount would be determined in the jury room. It was pretty much out of our hands at this point. There was certainly one skunk in the jury box I had to worry about—that damned Realtor—but even so, I felt pretty good as Judge Donner gave the jury their final instructions before dismissing them.

"You are not allowed to leave the jury room. If you have a question for the court, write it out on a piece of paper and have your jury foreperson sign his or her name. Knock on the door, and we will come open it slightly, just enough to take that piece of paper from you. There will be no other kind of communication with the jury until it has reached a verdict. When you have reached a verdict, knock on the door, and someone will come to the door. Have your foreperson say "We have reached a verdict" through the closed door. We will assemble as we are today and come knock on the door to get you so your verdict may be published.

"One other thing: within ten minutes or so, Ray will be bringing you the exhibits. The evidence is the province of the jury. This means you have a right to it. You will have everything. A television has also been set up in the jury room with a VCR. If you have any problems with that VCR or TV, please follow the same protocol by knocking and passing Ray a note. We will resolve any technical issues.

"If there aren't any other issues to go over, please leave your jury instructions in the courtroom, as there will be one signed copy awaiting you in the jury room. Thank you." When she concluded her instructions, Judge Donner dismissed the jury to start their deliberations. The jury had put in a grueling seven-and-a-half-hour day and was now confined to a small, hot room with broken air-conditioning and no blinds on the windows. Someone was supposed to install a set of blinds early that morning, but it never happened. The room was unbearable—hardly ideal conditions for the type of deliberations that would be taking place. The heat was stifling. Even with the windows open, the air was stagnant and thick.

After the jury retired from the courtroom, Gaebe brought up a concern to Judge Donner about a video deposition of Wishart and Chaffin in which they both had used some unsavory language to describe the workers on the farm. He wanted to edit out the parts where they referred to the African American workers as "coloreds." Judge Donner had already allowed them to take out Wishart's and Chaffin's references to Mexicans and Haitians, so this wasn't adding up. The discussion got rather heated, because there were various edited versions of this same deposition floating around as evidence. Judge Donner gave Gaebe the opportunity to get the tape edited one last time and to submit it into final evidence as exhibit 19. The only portion of the video that would exist would be dialogue about growing tomato plants.

On the first full day of deliberations, as the lawyers were going through the evidence with the court, the jury came back with a question regarding the science. They wanted to re-read the transcript of some of the witnesses' testimony, especially Dr. Brent's. This could be good or bad, depending on how they were looking at it. The judge denied their request and, as was usual in these types of cases, instructed the jury to go on their collective recollection. Given the lateness in the day when they asked this question, I was fairly certain they weren't coming back with a quick decision. This left everyone in limbo for the time being.

With the sun now setting, the conditions were really getting tough on the jurors. Judge Donner wanted to get them out of there with the hope that there would be blinds in the room by the time they returned the next day at 9:00 a.m. At the very least, she could make arrangements to keep the room cooler. There was no reasonable logic in keeping them late and forcing them into unfavorable circumstances for all involved parties. The last thing we needed was a hung jury.

Ray knocked on the jury room door and asked the jury to reassemble in the courtroom, where Judge Donner expressed her genuine concern for their comfort and well-being. Recognizing that they needed more time to deliberate, she explained that while her decision to let the jury go home was for their benefit, it was critical that they not discuss the details of the case with anyone else. That was solely for their deliberations when they were all together in the same room.

The following morning, the jury was instructed to go back to the jury room, where they would resume their assessment exactly where they'd left off the evening before. In the meantime, I had something of grave importance to bring to the court's immediate attention. I'd noticed a big conference between the DuPont and Pine Island Farms attorneys. The discussion concerned how Judge Donner had checked on the jury in the overheated room the day before. As Liz Russo had been involved in appellate decisions in the past that might have had some relevance to this, I felt compelled to mention that it was a technical violation of law for a judge to even open the jury room door or go into the room during deliberations. I offered on behalf of my client to waive any kind of appellate rights on this issue. Glynn agreed, while Gaebe needed to confer with his client. I suggested that, in the event Gaebe's client didn't waive his appellate rights on this point, that the judge ask the jury when they returned with their verdict if the one or two times Judge Donner opened the door to check on the heat, or the time Ray came in to deliver sandwiches, had any impact on the deliberations. Their response could potentially alleviate any problem if there was no waiver from Gaebe.

Glynn and I genuinely had no problem with Judge Donner's actions, and we certainly weren't worried about any impropriety, but we knew that once there was a verdict, each side would be looking for whatever it could find for an appeal, and something like this could easily mushroom into a big issue if not handled properly now. We didn't want the jury to go home, and for us to later have to deal with appellate problems. Nobody wanted that outcome, because that meant this trial would have been a big waste of time and money. Glynn made a good point when he said the jury could get more sensitive and nervous as time went on, so it was important for all subsequent communication with the jury to be conducted in the presence of counsel so as to avoid any additional issues.

Another unexpected situation arose that morning as well. Gaebe brought up what he thought was a press release handed to him that morning by DuPont's people. Chumbley quickly chimed in and corrected Gaebe, stating that it was actually a transcript of a BBC Radio broadcast reporting that, among other things, there was a lot of screaming and yelling and a five-to-one deadlock in the case—in the plaintiff's favor. It was amazing and impressive that DuPont had a transcript of a radio broadcast from Scotland that had occurred just hours before.

Gaebe was extremely concerned that while the jury was out, someone had gone to the press. He was worried that a party associated with the case was talking. Sometimes overhearing the screaming and yelling coming from a heated jury deliberation is unavoidable. In those types of situations, I actually don't want to hear what they're saying. It's all too subjective. But while listening might not be right, it also isn't wrong, and it certainly isn't tantamount to communicating.

As Gaebe spoke, however, it was clear that all the lawyers—myself included—shared the same concern. That is, until Chumbley said, "You're mentioned in here, Jim."

That was news to me.

I was shocked and angry at the thought, let alone the insinuation, that I would have talked to anyone, especially the media, during jury deliberations. I hadn't spoken to anyone, and I made damn sure everyone in that courtroom knew it.

Glynn stepped in and said that the reference to the five-to-one split was a particular cause for concern, because even if a lawyer overheard a lot of arguing, he would have a hard time deciphering a specific breakdown or split among the jury. One possible explanation for such a specific communication was that a juror had a connection to the outside world.

I agreed.

Chumbley then noted that the interview had been with Peter Attenborough, who was a client of a colleague of mine in London working on the Scottish cases. In the interview, Attenborough speculated on the jury split by saying, *"It appears . . ."* He wasn't being absolute. He was taking a shot in the dark. While my association with Attenborough, slight as it was, didn't look good, I certainly had nothing to do with that interview or his guessing game. Thankfully, Judge Donner saw it that way, too. She didn't find an appellate issue because there was no communication. If someone from the jury were communicating, there would have been a problem. If someone from counsel were listening, well, shame on them.

Glynn attempted to introduce the three-page transcript of the radio interview into evidence, but Judge Donner wasn't having it any more than she would have her personal grocery list being added in. She allowed the document for identification, and that was it.

Finally, Gaebe brought up a report that had appeared on the evening news the night before indicating that forty other children born with microphthalmia were either in the process of making claims or actually making claims as a result of Benlate use. Gaebe wanted to make sure the judge would ask the jury when the verdict was returned if they saw this report, which she agreed to do.

Sometime in the late morning the jury came back with a second question related to economic damages, which is usually a great sign for us. Generally, when you get an economic damages question, it means the jury has already resolved liability and will come back with a verdict in favor of the plaintiff within an hour or two. Unfortunately, they weren't as fast as I had expected. In fact, five hours went by without another word. Once again, we were back in limbo.

The Castillos weren't in the courtroom on this second day of deliberations. I'd had them there for closing arguments and felt it would be better if they waited things out in the comfort of my office, which was only ten minutes away. I assured them we would bring them back to the courtroom to be present for the reading of the verdict. The family was incredibly emotional that day. It had been almost six years since Johnny was born, and three long, intense years of litigation and waiting for justice. They needed some peace of mind that their son would be taken care of, and that answer was solely in the hands of this jury of their peers.

We received word that the jury had reached a verdict sometime around 5:00 p.m. I immediately called the Castillos to let them know so they could quickly make their way to the courthouse. So much time had passed after the asking of the economic question that we had no idea how it would go.

The atmosphere in the courtroom was intense. You could feel the anticipation in the air. Once again there was standing room only in the gallery. All three major networks were there to cover the verdict, as well as Court TV, which had been in the courtroom for the entire five weeks.

Judge Donner addressed the jury foreperson, Maria Miranda, and as was customary, she asked if the jury had reached a verdict.

"Yes we have, Your Honor."

"Would you please give your verdict to the clerk." Ms. Miranda handed the jury decision to the clerk, and the judge asked the clerk to publish it for the record.

"In the case of John Castillo, a minor; Donna Castillo; and Juan Castillo versus DuPont and Company and Pine Island Farms, we the jury return the following verdict.

"Was there negligence on the part of Pine Island Farms, which was the legal cause of damage to plaintiffs?

"Yes.

"Did the defendant DuPont place the fungicide Benlate on the market with a defect, which was a legal cause of damage to the plaintiffs?

"Yes.

"Was there negligence on the part of the defendant DuPont, which was the legal cause of damage to the plaintiffs?

"Yes.

"State the percentage of any responsibility that you charge to defendant Pine Island Farms:

"$20,000, which is 0.5 percent

"Defendant DuPont:

"$39,800."

Something was wrong; these numbers made no sense.

"Let me see that . . ." Judge Donner said as she angrily grabbed the document from the clerk. "It's $3,980,000."

It was a $4 million dollar decision for the plaintiff.

The courtroom erupted with cheers.

We had just made legal history.

When the clerk finished reading how the jury came up with their number and decision, as expected, Judge Donner polled them to make sure it had been a unanimous decision. She also asked if there was any interference from either her clerk or herself when they had knocked on the door to check on the air-conditioning during deliberations or while the jury was reaching its verdict. After they confirmed that there was no such interference, Judge Donner thanked the jury for their effort, for taking time away from their jobs, their families, and their busy lives. She reminded them that they had every right after the trial to choose who they spoke to and who they didn't. They were perfectly welcome not to speak with the lawyers on the case or the media. This was their choice alone to make.

As we closed things out, Judge Donner was extremely gracious in showing her gratitude to the jury. I was also grateful and very proud of the decision they made. I took a moment to enjoy the victory, even though everything in my experienced gut told me it would be short-lived. DuPont was surely going to file for an immediate appeal.

When court was adjourned, the atmosphere in our camp was really festive. We had been waiting for two days while the jury deliberated, and though we had hoped and prayed they'd deliver a verdict in our favor, one never really knows how these types of cases will end. Everyone was thrilled with the outcome—at least, everyone from the plaintiff's point of view.

Back then I liked to wear suspenders in court, especially during trial. It was a look that became synonymous with me, and, I suppose, Larry King. A lot of lawyers made fun of me for it, but I didn't care. In fact, I thought the suspenders were my good luck charm—and this time they really were, because somehow, against all odds, we had landed this verdict. It was nothing short of miraculous.

When I returned to my office that night, the atmosphere was euphoric. The first thing I did was light up a big cigar. My staff was passing around champagne, and all the major TV and cable networks were setting up for post-trial interviews. The energy was almost overwhelming.

After all the interviews I retreated back into the sanctity of my office. I leaned back in my soft, supple leather chair, put my feet up on my desk, and gazed at the Miami skyline. As I sat, I took it *all* in—the verdict, the victory, and the view.

I'd come a long way from my early days of practicing law, and yet moments like these never get old. As I was contemplating what had just happened, I was also thinking about what was to come next. But there would be time for that later. Right now I wanted to breathe in these few moments of peace I allowed myself that night.

The verdict was on the front page of the *Miami Herald* the following day and became international news because of its global implications. I received interview requests from all over the world, including from a very young Dan Abrams for Court TV; one from London's

*Night & Day* magazine, which is equivalent to the *New York Times Magazine*; and the top rated Austrian news magazine show, which I was told was like being profiled for *60 Minutes*. These news outlets were eager to hear from us and excited to help the Castillos share their story of triumphant conquest over DuPont.

It was all very exciting, and a bit daunting, too, because I knew round two of the fight would soon be upon us. As I predicted, it didn't take long for the defendants to file an appeal. The road ahead wasn't going to be a smooth one by any means; our win in Judge Donner's courtroom didn't guarantee a victorious outcome in another courtroom. Though we celebrated the milestone for everything it represented, we had a lot of work to do to ensure that our success stuck. There was no more time to bask in the media spotlight. We had to prepare for the next phase, and so we did.

# 21

WHEN A CASE like this comes to an end, some lawyers crash from the emotional and physical toll. Not me. For several weeks afterward, I was still incredibly energized—still eager to call witnesses and think about what I would have, could have, or should have done differently during the trial. My adrenaline was pumping as hard then as it had been before and during the trial.

Winning the case against DuPont was certainly a triumph, but it was by no means the end of the Castillos' legal nightmare. I was extremely satisfied that we had gone up against the behemoth and slew it, but we hadn't hauled its carcass off yet. You see, there's winning, and then there's collecting. Those two are worlds apart.

DuPont had brought in a total of ten lawyers from three firms, all fueled and fed by their fearless leader, Clem Glynn, who had proven to be a formidable opponent. But none of this had intimidated me. In fact, Glynn's presence only inspired me to work harder. I hadn't wanted to beat him so much as to win for the family—but if kicking

Glynn's ass in court came with that, then hey, I considered it a bonus, because he was such a sarcastic, egotistical bully who thought he could come in and steamroll us in court by picking on everyone and everything with his endless wiseass comments. He was very pomp-ous, thinking he was smarter than we were, but sometimes that type of ego can end up getting in your way.

Two months after the verdict, while the case was up on appeal, I certainly had no reason to talk to Glynn, and, frankly, there wasn't much about the guy that made me want to. You could have knocked me over with a feather when one unsuspecting afternoon my office phone rang, and it was Glynn.

Curious, I took the call. "What's up?" I said. Not even a proper hello. I didn't really want to pretend to have small talk.

Glynn began to speak, and for the first time since the case I heard a different side of the man I once viewed as Goliath. He was having a tough time getting over the loss. He sounded terrible, as if he were depressed—or worse. He told me he was "taking it very hard" and that this was the worst loss of his career.

When I heard those words, I sank in my chair. A lot of guys might have relished that moment of admission.

Not me.

I actually felt sorry for the guy. He was so downtrodden. I reminded Glynn how challenging a case this was and what a great job he did. He was fifty-one years old and perhaps looking backward at a time when I, having taken this one from him at age thirty-nine, was looking for-ward in my career.

I don't really know why he called that day, but it sure was a moment of unexpected weakness. This case was emotional for all of us. Instead of rubbing the poor guy's nose in it, though, I found myself consoling him.

"We were asking for $25 million and the jury gave us only $4 mil-lion. That has to be because of the work you did, Clem," I said, trying to reassure him that it wasn't a complete failure.

"Jim, you ought to know that at least five of the six jurors were going to give you the twenty-five. There was one holdout."

Years later, we learned from Judge Donner that after the jury had been discharged, they talked with her clerk, Ray, who confirmed what Glynn had said that day.

At the time, though, I wasn't sure how he knew this, but I was absolutely positive who the holdout was: yeah, that angry Realtor. I had wanted to get rid of him from the start, but we were out of challenges, so I had to let it go. He didn't want to be there, and he was going to make everyone else pay for it. Even little Johnny Castillo. And there was nothing I could do about it now. It made sense. That holdout must have been why the jury deliberated for two days—and why they stayed out for over five more hours after that economic damages question was asked. That explained it. They must have had to compromise, because this guy obviously wasn't interested in a payout like the one we were seeking. It was a classic compromise verdict.

I asked Glynn how he came to know about the jurors. I wondered if he had interviewed them after the trial, and he told me he had. I was surprised to hear that, but then again, it isn't uncommon to go back and look for something—*anything*—that could be used to overturn the verdict down the road. It could be something as simple as a juror reading a newspaper during the trial or talking to her spouse, who had some kind of relevant knowledge. These kinds of actions have the potential to sway a juror's opinion, and therefore the outcome of a case.

Glynn and I hung up, and I didn't hear from him again for well over a year. Our next communication—or, at least, attempt at communication—came just a few hours after the opinion came out on the appeal.

The appeal took place in Miami in the Third District Court of Appeals before a panel of three judges randomly selected out of the total court of nine. I asked Liz Russo to be my appellate attorney for the appeal, as she was very capable and very prepared to do so. She had a great deal of experience going into the case, so I thought she would do a fine job. Although we both prepared the brief together, Liz's main career focus was arguing appeals, so she took on that role here as well.

Unfortunately for us, DuPont got extremely lucky with the draw, getting the best three judges they could have hoped for—a trio of very conservative, blue-suited, like-minded, corporate-oriented individuals who could easily have fit into the DuPont camp. They may as well have been part of the DuPont team.

For the appeal, it was just me and my very capable appellate counsel against what seemed like half of Washington, DC. Lead counsel for DuPont was Ed Warren, the managing partner of the appellate division of Kirkland & Ellis, the biggest and most renowned appellate practice in the United States. Ed Warren was Ken Starr's replacement at Kirkland & Ellis when Starr left to lead President Clinton's impeachment proceedings. DuPont was so lawyered up for this oral argument they hired Arthur England, the former Chief Justice of the Florida Supreme Court to sit as third chair. He basically sat there for show.

As the appellant, DuPont argued first. Right out of the box, the panel's questions for DuPont were very friendly. It seemed that the court was favorable to their position, but it wasn't until Liz began arguing that we really felt the dagger to the heart.

At one point, astonishingly, a jurist on the panel asked Liz, "Ms. Russo, this is the nineties; don't you think four million dollars is a lot of money to give to a kid with no eyes who is essentially going to live a normal life?"

That's when we knew we had a real problem.

When someone thinks it's normal to live life with no eyes—or, worse, wants to attach a low dollar value to the pain, suffering, and hardship associated with such a condition simply because he can't fathom what it would be like, I get angry. Really angry. I also knew we were fucked. Clearly, these judges were biased toward DuPont.

While we were awaiting the decision on the appeal, we had started to vigorously pursue twenty-nine cases on behalf of children in Scotland who were affected by Benlate. As it turned out, we were doing so right on DuPont's home turf. We had originally attempted to get these cases tried in West Virginia because we had local counsel who believed we could get a fair shake in their state, since DuPont had a large plant there that manufactured Benlate. But unfortunately, after we filed suit there, we were kicked out and sent packing to Delaware. We had no choice in the matter. Since these children were not from the United States, we had to file in the defendant's state of incorporation, and so we did.

When we showed up in Delaware for our first hearing on the defense's first motion (to kick the cases entirely out of the United States on the basis of *forum non conveniens*), we realized just what home-court advantage really looks like. As we pulled up to our hotel in Wilmington—called what else but the DuPont—we were greeted by banners celebrating the company's bicentennial. They were flying from every lamppost in the city—even the ones in front of the courthouse. *200 Years of DuPont!* They were inescapable.

When we went into court for the hearing, we were greeted by yet another set of high-powered attorneys, including David Boies from Boies, Schiller & Flexner; Pat Leigh, the best defense litigator from Crowell & Moring; and three other unnamed grayheads. Their sole purpose was to oust these families from the courts of Delaware, and send them back to Scotland, which they succeeded in doing, at least temporarily. We appealed that ruling to the Delaware Supreme Court and got it reversed. This was the first of three appeals these plaintiffs had to endure. The second involved the Delaware trial court dismissing the Scottish families' suits on statute of limitations grounds. DuPont argued that the statute of limitations began at the birth of the children. We argued that it began when the children found out that the cause of their conditions was Benlate. We were right. Again, we got a trial court ruling in favor of DuPont reversed by the Delaware Supreme Court.

The last appeal involved the trial court excluding two of our scientists, which in effect gutted our case. This last appeal was a split decision (between three judges), which meant that we then had to go back in front of a full panel of five judges at the Delaware Supreme Court. And that was definitely not good for us. As if that wasn't enough to contend with, one of the Supreme Court judges on the full panel was named DuPont. Obviously, he had to recuse himself from the case. And yes, he was related to the family. Before leaving, however, he did have the privilege of handpicking a chancellor to take his place, someone we guessed was a buddy of his from law school or some other close connection. After that, we knew we had no chance of winning the appeal in Delaware. I'm not saying the system was rigged, but there certainly was a lot of love for DuPont in the community. We were now on life support, but still alive.

During the appellate process at the Third District Court of Appeals in Florida, DuPont did two notable and important things. First, it took Benlate off the market permanently. It did this despite Benlate's being DuPont's number-one-selling agricultural product in the world at the time, with sales over $1 billion. Second, but actually taking place before Benlate's removal from the market, DuPont finally undertook more realistic scientific studies on benomyl. The company performed a series of ten pharmacokinetic studies intended to determine what exactly happens to benomyl when it gets into the body. One of these pharmacokinetic studies involved autoradiography, which is a process whereby radioactive isotopes are attached to molecules of the chemical in order to trace where it travels within the body.

At the same time DuPont was doing its studies, we commissioned our own study at TNO, the Netherlands Organization for Applied Scientific Research. Our study involved putting Benlate on the skin of the arms and hands of male subjects to determine how much got into the bloodstream. Of course, we couldn't do this with pregnant women.

While these studies were in progress, the Third District Court of Appeals issued its opinion. Unfortunately for us, it was not a good one. The opinion reversed the decision of the trial court, with no opportunity for another trial. The decision was not a typical appellate decision, as the court undertook to determine its own facts when its job was solely to interpret the law. The appellate decision made no sense legally, and smelled of politics. It was extremely disappointing, and, needless to say, the Castillos and I were devastated when we lost this appeal. We were outgunned politically and otherwise. DuPont got a damn good draw, and there was nothing we could do about it but attempt to take the case to the next level if that's what the Castillos wanted to do. We were now on life support in both Delaware and Florida.

I wasn't in my office when Glynn called the day the appellate opinion was handed down. I just received a message from my secretary that he had called. I was certain he wanted to gloat about the decision, with a great big boisterous "I told you so." I was in no mood to deal with that kind of braggadocio—not then, and frankly not ever.

I didn't bother to return the call.

# 22

IN THE AFTERMATH of the appellate decision, the Castillos and I had a limited period of time in which to decide whether we would try to get this case to the Florida Supreme Court. Doing so wouldn't be easy, as the process is discretionary, and the court takes very few of these types of cases. It would require filing a petition for review known as a *writ of certiorari*. The chances of the Florida Supreme Court taking our case were somewhere between one in seventy-five and one in a hundred. With odds like that, we had to give some serious thought to letting the case go. If the case went forward, it wouldn't require any further testimony from the Castillos, but it would require extra time and money, lots of patience, and even more pressure and emotional stress on the family.

These are never easy decisions. We knew in our heart of hearts we were right. Having invested so much time, money, and emotion into the matter already, we had to decide if it made sense to take the shot. Personally, I was not prepared to stop until we had breathed our last breath. But at the end of the day, this wasn't about me.

•    •    •

In a case like this, a victory at the state Supreme Court is very difficult. For that matter, winning *any* case at the state Supreme Court is tough. In essence, an ultimate victory is a two-step process that requires two wins. The first step requires the filing of the *writ of certiorari* which is nothing more than a request to the court asking them to simply hear our case let alone rule in our favor. The second step in the process (if you are lucky enough to get past the first step), is to file a brief on the merits of the case.

The filing of the writ, receipt of the opposition's response, and the time burned waiting for a ruling at step one takes up to a year or longer. If you're successful at this level, there are still no guarantees of an ultimate victory other than the simple right to argue the facts and the law of your case to the state Supreme Court. If the court grants your writ, then, and only then, will you get to step two. At step two, you are basically starting over, as if pleading your case for the first time, whereby you have to re-educate another court and try to convince them to overturn the Third District Court of Appeals and reinstate the verdict rendered by the jury. Just like the writ, which is rarely granted, your likelihood of success on the merits is also limited.

The low level of success in getting a *writ of certiorari* granted in a case as complicated as ours is compounded by a ten-page limit in which to get in all your facts and law to compel the court to hear your case. If the writ is granted, then you get to brief the case on the merits subject to a fifty page limit. Imagine, fifty pages to pack in an entire six-week-long trial that involved over five hundred bankers boxes of evidence and the testimony of dozens of witnesses that testified at trial.

The decision whether to proceed or not was going to be very difficult. I was getting very concerned for the Castillos. It had already been a long six years since Donna Castillo first showed up at my office. The family had suffered through the extreme stress and pressure that comes with preparing for a trial, including but not limited to, testifying, cross-examination and the related personal attacks. That was followed by the exhilarating high of winning the six-week-long trial, including two full days of roller-coaster jury deliberations. The family then endured the pain and embarrassment of the jury verdict being taken away by the Third District Court of Appeals. At this point, serious consideration had to be given to not putting this family through any more pain. I could literally feel the agony that the Castillo family had been through.

Even though the odds were heavily stacked against us, I was not ready to quit. After much soul searching and extensive conversations with the Castillos, the decision was ultimately made to proceed with the *writ of certiorari*. Neither the Castillos nor I were prepared to give up the hope that Johnny would have the option of having the financial means to get the proper schooling and assistance that his life required.

We filed our writ, received responses from the defendants, and now we could only hope and pray that we would beat the overwhelming odds against us. I was mentally preparing myself for how I would break the agonizing news to the Castillos in the extremely likely event of an adverse decision from the court.

After many months of waiting we finally received the decision on our writ.

Lo and behold, almost a year later, the state Supreme Court decided to take the case as one of great public importance. The court considered our case to have great public importance because it involved if, how, and when science is admitted by trial court judges in Florida.

We won step one!

We now had to fully brief and argue the merits of the case to the Florida Supreme Court. This is the first positive news we had gotten in a long time. We still had a long way to go. Once we got this chance, however, we were able to start breathing on our own again. By no means were we in the Promised Land, but we were still alive and kicking.

* * *

During the briefing process, we got the results of DuPont's scientific studies and ours. The results were very favorable for us. Unfortunately, these studies would not be admissible in the state Supreme Court case, because they are not allowed to review evidence outside of the original Castillo trial transcript. Both their study and ours showed that we were 100 percent right, and the Third District Court of Appeals was 100 percent wrong. Without exception, every subject in our TNO study who had had benomyl placed on his skin was urinating out its metabolites. What this meant was that the chemical definitely got into the bloodstream, passed through the kidneys, and was ultimately secreted out as urine.

That was good, but even more astounding were the results of DuPont's studies. When we received the series of the pharmacokinetic studies from DuPont, one was suspiciously missing from the numbered series: the autoradiography report, which showed that the chemical would accumulate in various tissues and organs—in particular the kidneys, which had the second-highest amount of accumulation, a result that tied right into the findings of our own studies. But the most amazing discovery of all was that the highest concentration of the chemical was found in the uveal tract of the eyes!

DuPont shot themselves in the foot, and in the process proved that we were right all along. While I was happy to have the data, it wouldn't help the Castillos.

# 23

WHILE WE WERE in the briefing process at the Florida Supreme Court, my firm received a letter from Greg Gaebe that stated if we dropped all appeals, Pine Island Farms would not seek court costs against the Castillo family. These assessable costs would be well into the hundreds of thousands of dollars. When the appellate decision came down, we had gone from being winners to being losers, which gave Gaebe's clients the right to collect court costs from the Castillo family if they wanted to. In reality, a company such as DuPont or Pine Island Farms would very rarely seek to recover costs against the family of a blind child. Imagine that headline.

In any event, Ana Rivero, who was still very green in these types of matters, took it upon herself to call the Castillos and share the contents of the letter without explaining the reality of what it meant. If I had made that call, I would have explained that DuPont would never attempt to collect money from them, and then I'd do my best to put the family at ease so we could properly continue with our appeal.

Ana did none of that. Instead, she instilled fear in the Castillos, who couldn't afford to pay a sum like that.

One afternoon, Ana walked into my office with a scared look on her face. She was pale; she looked as if she were about to drop a nuclear bomb on me.

And she was.

"I've got bad news, Jim," she said, her voice shaking.

"What bad news?"

"The Castillos want to drop the appeal."

"What do you mean they want to drop the appeal? Why would they do that?" I asked.

This was the first time Ana told me about Gaebe's letter. I expressed to her how ridiculous that attempt was, because obviously Pine Island would never do that.

"I need to talk to them right away," I said.

"I don't think it will do much good. They seem very adamant about dropping the appeal." Ana was practically in tears.

"I don't understand," I said. And I didn't. I was completely baffled; how could we have gotten this far only to have the family bail out now?

"You know Juan; he's an accountant. He's very conservative and doesn't want to take any financial risk at all," she said.

I was fuming. I was so livid I couldn't see straight. My blood pressure went off the charts. Doing something like this was as inexperienced as it gets. After all the Castillos had been through, how could Ana possibly have put them through yet another emotional trauma? It was so unnecessary, and totally senseless. This family had endured so much already.

I should have fired Ana on the spot, but I didn't, because I still had the twenty-nine other cases pending in Delaware, and she was the only person in my office other than me who had any knowledge of those cases.

I called Juan and Donna and did my best to explain the realities of the situation. Despite my best efforts, Juan still didn't want to take the chance and affirmed my worst fear—they wanted to drop the case.

I asked Juan to allow me one week to work something out with Pine Island Farms to make sure they wouldn't come after the family for costs. I gave them every assurance that nothing would happen during that window of time.

After hanging up with the Castillos and getting over my barely controllable frustration, I called Gaebe and asked him if he wanted to play a round of golf at the Riviera Country Club in Coral Gables, where we were both members. This was neutral territory, unrelated to law and not on anyone's home court. Knowing that Gaebe was cagey, I had to be careful about how I handled this delicate situation. I couldn't just wing this; I needed a plan. I decided that the only real chance we had was not to address the issue head-on with Gaebe but instead to do it surreptitiously after a round of golf and a couple of drinks.

Our outing took place on a clear, cool Saturday morning. We played eighteen holes and talked about our children, sports, other members of the club—anything but the Castillos. When we finished our game, we retired to the clubhouse and downed a couple of cold beers. It was probably sometime around our third beer when I nonchalantly said, "By the way, Gaebe, why did you send that fucked-up costs letter to the Castillos?"

"You know, it's just standard bullshit, Jim," he said.

"You scared the fuck out of my clients for no good reason."

"I didn't mean to scare anyone."

"How about I cap Pine Island Farms' potential damages at $1 million regardless of any appeals for agreeing to drop any claim for costs, so these people can stop pissing in their pants," I proposed.

"That sounds like a good deal."

"Thanks a lot, Greg. There's no reason to scare them after all they've been through." Little did he know they were about to drop the entire case, and in getting him to agree to this proposal I had just saved all our efforts from being flushed down the toilet.

First thing Monday morning I sent Gaebe a letter confirming our deal and let the family know the good news.

Mission accomplished.

Thank God.

# 24

THE DAY OF oral arguments was surreal. We had been through so much already, from the trial, to the court of appeals, to getting the Florida Supreme Court to grant our writ. Now it was time for us to present our case to the state's highest court. Each side had a grand total of thirty minutes to argue their case. Not much time, considering the great public importance and complexity of the case.

It was very difficult to tell from the oral argument how the court would rule. All the justices were active during the process; asking in-depth questions on the critical issues. It was clear that the court had great interest in our case. Unlike the Third District Court of Appeals which was clearly biased for DuPont, the Supreme Court was very neutral. This was a breath of fresh air after what we had been through in our last appeal, and gave us some level of optimism.

The normal wait to get a decision from the Florida Supreme Court after oral argument is typically six to nine months. Unfortunately for the Castillos, our wait time was not the norm. One year passed, then two, without a peep. It wasn't until two-and-a-half-years after the oral argument that we finally got the decision. In total, we were at the Supreme Court for nearly five years!

I vividly remember the day I got the decision, because I was on my way back from one of my trips to the UK to visit the Scottish families involved in the twenty-nine cases still pending in Delaware. I was riding in the back of a black London cab with two of my kids, who had traveled with me on this particular trip, when I received a call from Lynn Holtzman, one of my associates, telling me the Supreme Court had ruled. At first I couldn't understand what she was saying because of her absolute jubilance.

"Lynn, calm down. I can't make out what you're saying."

"We won!"

"We won?" I asked.

"Yes, we won!" she shouted into the phone.

I asked her if she had read through the entire document to be certain that the decision was what it appeared to be. Sometimes—though not often—the opinion isn't what it appears to be on the surface. I wanted definitive confirmation.

"Yes, Jim. I've read it and it's over. You did it. We won on all issues."

I was elated and relieved. Against great odds, the Supreme Court had reinstated our verdict in its entirety. This win at the Florida Supreme Court was a landmark decision that would shape how trial courts admitted scientific evidence for years to come. The decision was over forty pages long, and, page by page, it completely undressed and dismantled DuPont. The decision was not simply of great public importance. It was monumental!

I could hardly wait to call the Castillos to share this great news. I was so excited I could barely dial the phone. It had been just over ten years and this grueling marathon had finally come to a victorious end. I felt a whirlwind of emotions—for the Castillos, for myself, for the trial judge who had been overturned, and for the good that will come from this decision for so many people going forward. Probably the greatest satisfaction I got from the entire case was hearing Donna cry when I told her we had finally won, once and for all.

"Donna, I've got some very good news . . ."

"Don't tell me we won," she said, sounding somewhat scared.

"Then I won't tell you, but we did," I said, trying to bring a little levity to this incredibly emotional moment for both of us.

And as the news sank in, Donna tried to catch her breath in between sobs. All she could ask was "Is it *really* over? Oh my God, I can't believe it."

After I broke the news to the Castillos, I got onto the plane back to Miami feeling higher than the aircraft was flying. I thought about Clem Glynn and wondered whether I should return the call he'd made when DuPont won the appeal at the Third District Court of Appeals almost five years ago. Donna Castillo had walked into my office for the first time in June 1993. It wasn't until July 10, 2003, that we finally got word from the Supreme Court of Florida. For a brief moment I thought I'd give Clem a ring as if no time had passed at all and say, "Hi, Clem. Just returning your call from a few years back," and then revel a little over our win.

I poured myself a scotch as I watched the clouds float by at 39,000 feet and thought to myself, "Why bother?" There was far more dignity and grace in simply saying nothing and allowing the court's decision to do my talking.

This was the end of the Castillo case for DuPont. They would finally have to pay, and by this time enough interest had accrued during all the appeals that the payment was for just under $7 million. When all was said and done, the family received more than $4 million. It wasn't the $25 million we almost got at trial. However, it was enough money for the Castillos to live as happily as possible and to send their son to Perkins or a similar school for the blind. After the trial, the Castillos moved to Massachusetts, where Juan continued his career as an accountant and Donna continued to care for their son.

Our success paid dividends for the Castillo family in other ways, too, as Johnny was able to fine-tune his other senses and become a gifted singer and musician. Ten years after the trial, the Boston Red Sox invited him to sing the national anthem on Easter Sunday at a Red Sox home game. One of my only regrets is not finding out about him singing until after it happened.

Our case was the first jury verdict in history affirmed on appeal against a chemical company for causing a birth defect where the plaintiff actually won. However, the real rewards for my team and me in winning the Castillo case came when DuPont finally took Benlate off the market in 2000 and in knowing the Castillos would finally be able to get on with their lives. Having a hand in both outcomes was extremely humbling and gratifying.

# 25

THE RESULTS OF our third and final appeal at the Delaware Supreme Court came in shortly after the Florida Supreme Court reinstated the *Castillo* decision. Unfortunately, the Delaware Trial Court had ruled against us on select scientific issues (that severely hurt those cases) prior to the Florida Supreme Court decision. In fact, during the two-and-a-half-year wait for a decision from the Florida Supreme Court, the Delaware trial court judge asked us repeatedly when the Florida Supreme Court was going to hand down their decision. Of course, we didn't have an answer for that. If we did, and had the Florida Supreme Court ruled before the Delaware Trial Court, I believe things would have turned out much differently in Delaware.

Despite the fact that the third appeal in Delaware severely hampered the position of the twenty-nine Scottish families, I knew once and for all I had finally come of age in the eyes of DuPont. Normally, DuPont would take a very harsh stance, but after ten years of litigation on the Castillo case, the company had developed an odd respect for me. It knew, without a doubt, that I wouldn't stop until these cases were 100 percent toast.

Although he fully understood this about me, Bill Gordon, DuPont's head of litigation, gave me a call anyway. He was trying to feel me out, hoping I would pull the plug on the cases after we lost two of our scientists. Of course, he knew that would never happen, but he had to try.

"Do you have any idea what your plans are for the Scottish families?" he asked, wishing I'd say "Game, set, and match."

"I guess you and I will be doing business for another five years," I said, letting him know I wasn't going anywhere.

"Maybe there's a way we can work this out," he said.

The Scottish families ultimately settled with DuPont for millions of dollars—hardly the hundreds of millions I had hoped for, but enough money to allow each family to move on with their lives.

This was the end of my personal saga with DuPont.

Ten years and over $1 million in costs later, we were able to get the Castillos and the Scottish families paid, recoup our costs from DuPont, and finally earn some fees. By this time, however, I was making crazy amounts of money and was no longer seen as a neophyte in this arena. I started getting a lot of inquiries from people all over the world. Today we represent a broader base of clients, such as tax-whistleblowers, a variety of environmental cases, tobacco cases, and a whole host of other catastrophic litigation. I am proud to say that as of the publication of this book, we have the largest inventory of asbestos and tax-whistleblower cases in the country. It certainly pays the bills. However, I still never count the money we win until the check comes in and clears.

In 1997 Trial Lawyers for Public Justice (now known simply as Public Justice) named me a national finalist for Trial Lawyer of the Year because of my work in *Castillo*. I didn't win, but it was an honor to be nominated by such a prestigious organization.

• • •

I often marvel at how life always comes around full circle. One of the most important and sentimental moments for me during the trial was when my ten-year-old son, James, watched my closing argument from a premier seat in the courtroom. I don't know whether or not this was an inspiration for him, but in 2013, nearly twenty years after the initial Castillo verdict, James became an attorney and a member of the Florida Bar. On the day he passed his bar exam, I couldn't help but think about my father and his great accomplishment in becoming the first college graduate in our family. Now, here was my son—someone who could have chosen any profession—consciously deciding to follow in my footsteps.

My son Andrew, who is the same age as Johnny Castillo, started law school in the fall of 2016. His strength and courage is a source of great inspiration to me. My daughter, Alexis, graduated college in 2015 from a top business school in Boston. She has an undying passion for technology and charity work. Her dream is to someday run her own foundation that will help fulfill her life goal of helping people in need. My son Dmitri who is five years old, speaks four languages already, and, like all my children, is surely destined to do amazing things with his life. Last year was also a charm as my newest addition, my son Mateo, was born. I hope the work I do makes the world a better place, not only for my children, and some day their children, but for all of us.

In August 2015 my son James participated in his first jury trial with me as an associate from the Ferraro Law Firm. The case was *Roy Taylor-vs-Georgia Pacific*. I hadn't tried a case in several years and was feeling a bit rusty, but I decided to take this one on because the client was a very good human being and the case involved dealing with a difficult set of circumstances and facts that were very hard to prove. I also wanted to take James through his first trial and show him what I believed was the right way to perform in a courtroom. In just under two weeks, we received a verdict for the Taylors in the amount of $17,175,000—a verdict that was *not* appealed. Unlike in the Castillo case, I knew we won this time when we received a jury question that simply read, "Can we have a calculator? ☺"

Hands down, this was by far the best jury question I had ever received in my entire career.

Just as Court TV covered the *Castillo trial* from inside the courtroom, CVN, the Courtroom View Network, now televises every jury trial in the state of Florida. Much to my surprise, CVN named me the 2015 Florida Trial Lawyer of the Year because of the *Taylor trial*.

For me, it was the experience of a lifetime and truly an honor to be a part of my son's first trial. How extraordinary it was to share this victory with him. It gave me such great pride to see how he embraced our clients and shared their emotions throughout the trial. His compassion and wisdom astounded me. When the verdict was read, all the pent-up feelings and anxiety faded away as the Taylors and James embraced each other in an ocean of tears.

As a trial lawyer, I know how challenging it can be to succeed in law. I can't put words to the sentiment I held for my son James during that trial as I watched him launch his own career, knowing he has what it takes to be even better than I will ever be in a courtroom.

As for me, it's been twenty years since *Castillo*, and the thing that still sits heavy on my mind is that corporations like DuPont, tobacco manufacturers, and pharmaceutical companies are still hiding behind the shield of junk science. It's so unfair to the public that a corporation can test their products however they see fit; submit that science to governmental agencies such as the EPA to get a license to sell those products to us, the unsuspecting public; and then, when things go wrong, claim that the very same science is nothing but junk. This is one of the frailties of our legal system, a cancer developed through many years of big money lobbying to keep this sham in place. My goal going forward is to educate the public about this travesty of justice and to create enough public awareness to get a federal law passed that reads as follows: "Any scientific studies or information submitted by anyone to a governmental agency for purposes of licensing a product shall be admissible in a court of law."

I am now on a mission to get a bill sponsored and passed through the House of Representatives and the Senate that calls for this very important change in our legal system. What happened to Johnny Castillo could have happened to any of us. Without change, history will continue to repeat itself.